The Theatre Student
DIRECTING

THE THEATRE STUDENT SERIES

George Schaefer directing a scene from "Saint Joan" for NBC-TV Hallmark Hall of Fame.
NBC Photo

The Theater Student

DIRECTING

Paul Kozelka

PUBLISHED BY
RICHARDS ROSEN PRESS, INC.
NEW YORK, N.Y. 10010

Standard Book Number: 8239-0148-3
Library of Congress Catalog Card Number: 68-21662
Dewey Decimal Classification: 792

Published in 1968 by Richards Rosen Press, Inc.
29 East 21st Street, New York City, N.Y. 10010

Revised Edition

Manufactured in the United States of America

CONTENTS

To E.A.B.

ABOUT THE AUTHOR

PAUL KOZELKA has had a noteworthy career in education for the theatre. Associated for a number of years with the Department of Speech and Theatre Arts of Teachers College, Columbia University, he became Acting Chairman in 1963. Since the Drama Workshop was inaugurated in 1947, he has produced and directed more than eighty-one plays.

Among professional affiliations, he was President of the American Education Theatre Association in 1965 and served as Vice-President and Program Chairman of the Association's 1964 Convention, and was National Director of the Children's Theatre Conference (a division of the Association) in 1955-57. He is a former member of the Executive Committee and of the Board of Directors of the American National Theatre and Academy and also served on the Nominating and Editorial Committees. In 1966 he was consultant for the school system of Fort Lauderdale, Florida, to help draw up an exemplary program in speech and theatre for the junior and senior high schools. As a member of the Coordinating Committee for 1966 of the Speech Association of America, he worked to promote cooperation between the Association and related organizations.

Among his publications are articles for *Players Magazine, Dramatics Magazine,* and the *Encyclopaedia Britannica.* He has also written guides for screen versions of *Othello* and *Richard III,* an introduction to four plays by Bernard Shaw, and edited *Fifteen American One-Act Plays.*

A frequent speaker on theatrical subjects, he has addressed groups at the Language Arts Conference of St. Augustine College, Raleigh, North Carolina; the American Embassy in London, England; the New York State Theatre Festival Association, and many others. He was the recipient of the Eaves Junior Award in 1963.

Putting on a play or musical should be an enjoyable task for everyone concerned. To make it an educative experience as well requires certain preparation and a special mental attitude by the director. This book, and the entire series of which it is designed to be the first, will attempt to explain the process by which play production can serve an artistic and educational purpose.

The theatre experience is a vital one today. It brings together a group of people for a single reason: to understand a playwright's interpretation of a fragment of life and to enjoy a vicarious experience. This experience can happen in front of a television set, too, but being with a number of other people in the same theatre satisfies a deep gregarious instinct in man. Even more important is the pleasure of being face to face with living performers who are presenting a unique, not mechanized entertainment.

What does participation in theatre hold for students? For those who act, it provides the challenge of understanding a playwright's mental processes, of creating original characterizations, and of learning the most exacting type of self-imposed discipline. For the technical crews responsible for the visual aspects of the production, it provides an opportunity to design and create settings, costumes, and lighting effects not in miniature and for the future, but in a life-size laboratory where results will be tested immediately by living actors and a living audience. For the publicity crew, it means creating original ideas and implementing them, and it means acquiring actual, not theoretical experience with people, money, and accounting.

In today's world ideas are at a premium, and working in the theatre with all its challenges and requirements can develop the habit of approaching every problem in a critical, creative, and original way.

The director especially must be creative, because each play is a unique creation that must be understood and interpreted on its own terms and by its own standards. So, for the teacher-director, play production can keep him artistically alive. But further, he will derive immense satisfaction from watching students develop in self-respect, critical appreciation, sense of responsibility, and ability to employ their imaginations.

This book in the series *The Theatre Student* is written for the man or woman, teacher, student, or civic leader who is going to direct his first play. The processes described are based on tested practices and have been successfully used by experienced directors. The series is called *The Theatre Student* because anyone who works in theatre must forever remain a student, learning something new each moment, keeping a flexible, open mind that can absorb ideas from all sources, and maintaining a lively curiosity about people, new plays, and social and political events.

The director's attitude is paradoxical: At certain times he must be an authoritarian and a dictator, and at others he must be a democratic group leader who evokes ideas and inspires self-reliance. He must know his group members well so that he can adjust his methods according to the person and the moment. Since he is in a position of power, he must learn to use that power for the good of the play and not for his own aggrandizement. He may believe, for instance, that Mary Smith's personality would benefit from playing the lead and that she should be rewarded for the committee work she has done, but he also knows she is not a good enough actress to convince an audience. As an artist, therefore, he places Mary in a small role and gives the lead to the best actress he can find. Mary Smith's personality can benefit from other experiences provided by the school; and Mary herself might be embarrassed and the whole show suffer if she were given the lead for humanitarian reasons.

As an artist-leader, the director must plan the production in every detail so that he will have a solution for any problem that might arise; but as a group leader he must inspire ideas in others so that they may grow as people. The group process takes longer, but the results are worth working for in morale and in artistic merit as well.

The material in this book is arranged in a roughly chronological order. The problems in play directing are discussed as they arise. Many of the points I make are illustrated by quoting from the play *Lawyer Lincoln,* by Betty Smith and Chase Webb, which is reproduced in its entirety in the Appendix for easy reference. *Lawyer Lincoln* is a stimulating play and should be within the abilities of a beginning group interested in working on good material. The Appendix also contains lists of short and long plays, musicals, and plays for an audience of children. Some of the shows listed are more ambitious than others. The director or the play selection committee has the big job of going through catalogues and then reading many plays before choosing the one to present. The more plays a director knows, the more easily he can find one suitable for his group.

This book and the entire series should explain the first steps in play production. Experience in actual production will lead to advanced steps with ambitious shows to enrich the lives of participants and community alike.

FOREWORD

Our century has seen the role of the director assume increasing importance with each passing decade. We have come to appreciate the work of a Constantin Stanislavsky, a Max Reinhardt, a Tyrone Guthrie, or an Elia Kazan as great theatre artists who learned their craft and art in the amateur and professional theatre. We know now that a great play doesn't just "happen" on stage, but is the weaving together in an artistic unity the talents, visions, and skills of many workers under the intelligent, planned, sensitive, and skilled guidance or leadership of *one* artist, the director. His imagination and vision give it unity.

This is a far cry from the belief that exists in many quarters that "just any one can direct the school play." This is a sentiment that I still find as I travel through the country, examining the status of the theatre arts in our schools. What is the novice to do when responsibility for directing the play falls to his lot? He knows that he is unprepared for so important an undertaking, and often doesn't even know how to begin, except to "muddle through." There are many fine books on play direction, but they almost without exception seem too involved, complex, or advanced for his needs.

To fill this gap and to provide a handbook on play direction for the beginner, Paul Kozelka has written this book, the first of a series on theatre arts. He deserves our thanks. He is eminently qualified to write such a volume, for it comes out of his own experience, both as teacher and director. Paul knows the needs of the secondary school play director. He is a past director of the Children's Theatre Conference, and served on the governing board of the Secondary School Theatre Conference.

I have been fortunate to work with him in these organizations, to see productions he has directed, and to work with some of his students. There is no better way to describe Paul Kozelka than in his own words concerning the theatre educator: "an alert

15

person, a sensitive teacher, and an imaginative, creative theatrician." I personally am grateful to him for writing this book and I wholeheartedly recommend it to all who are directing a play for the first time and to all those who are teaching students eager to become directors. It is sound in theory and thorough in treatment.

William H. Cleveland, Jr.
Director, Dramatics, George School, Pennsylvania
Director of Secondary School Theatre Conference,
    a Division of AETA

The Theatre Student
DIRECTING

PROLOGUE

Some people think that the director in the theatre is a 20th-century development. But this is not true. Every play that was ever produced had a director or manager to interpret the play and to tell the actors when and where to move.

In the golden age of Greece, Aeschylus and Sophocles wrote the plays, coached the actors, trained the chorus in singing and dancing, and even painted scenery. The playwright is sometimes a good director, but usually he is too much interested in hearing the words to pay enough attention to the stage picture. Sometimes he is too exhausted from writing to have the energy to direct. But the Greeks had long rehearsal periods, and the playwrights knew better than anyone else what effects they wanted. Furthermore the writers knew their audiences very well, and they understood the ritual nature of the theatre. The audience came for a religious experience and to see their myths reenacted.

The Greek chorus had a recognized place in the proceedings, and the three main actors could assume many characters by changing masks and costumes. The director's function was to integrate chorus and principals and to understand his audience's frame of mind and threshold of belief.

In medieval days a stage manager carefully organized the rehearsals and performances of the large groups of amateur actors required by the cycle plays of England and France. The stage manager may also have been the author, but we cannot prove this. The plays grew out of Biblical accounts and never reached the poetic levels of Greek drama, so the performers concentrated on broad, literal effects to please their peasant audiences. Decisions as to how much horseplay the devils could engage in, how long Herod should rant and rave, and how drunk Noah should appear were probably left up to the individual actor, but the continuity of the performance depended on the stage manager.

That free form of Renaissance improvised entertainment known as *commedia dell' arte* was performed by tightly knit

A scene from Oedipus Rex directed by Bert De Rose at Wilbur H. Lynch High School, Amsterdam, New York. Greek tragedies are particularly appropriate for outdoor production because of their massive emotions and hero-size actions.

companies under one leader. His job was to prepare the scenario for each performance and to keep his company at top performance level. The actors were so proficient in their individual specialties of pantomime, recitation, song, dance, or acrobatics that they probably never rehearsed an entire production, but instead polished their individual talents to perfection.

In Elizabethan days, the playwright usually directed his own plays. Shakespeare probably had a lot to say about processions, costumes, and business for the performers, just as his voice was heard in management policies. It must be remembered that Shakespeare's actors had a strong tradition of rhetorical acting behind them and could create a characterization with little outside help. Malvolio, for example, was a familiar type who could be reproduced readily on the stage. Today, the young actor must be introduced to the life and times of the play so that he can understand the characters and comprehend the meaning of what they say.

The Master of the Revels was an important figure at this time. He produced the Court Masques and coached his amateur actors from among the courtiers in speaking and dancing. He supervised costumes, properties, musical numbers, groupings, and entrances and exits.

During the Restoration period and the 18th century authors read their plays to assembled companies to be sure of a single interpretation. The authors often were on hand during the rehearsal period to give directions and settle arguments, but the prompter or book holder took care of the mechanics of rehearsal.

In the 19th century companies of actors led by actor-managers toured the United States and Great Britain. These actor-managers were often star performers, more interested in personal success than in the total impact of the play. Acting reached a high level of technical brilliance, but the plays became vehicles rather than artistic statements. It was an actor's theatre rather than the writer's theatre it had been in classical Greece and in the Elizabethan period.

Bravura performances by glamorous stars kept the theatre here and abroad full of delighted customers, but they angered certain serious theatre workers, among them Johann Wolfgang

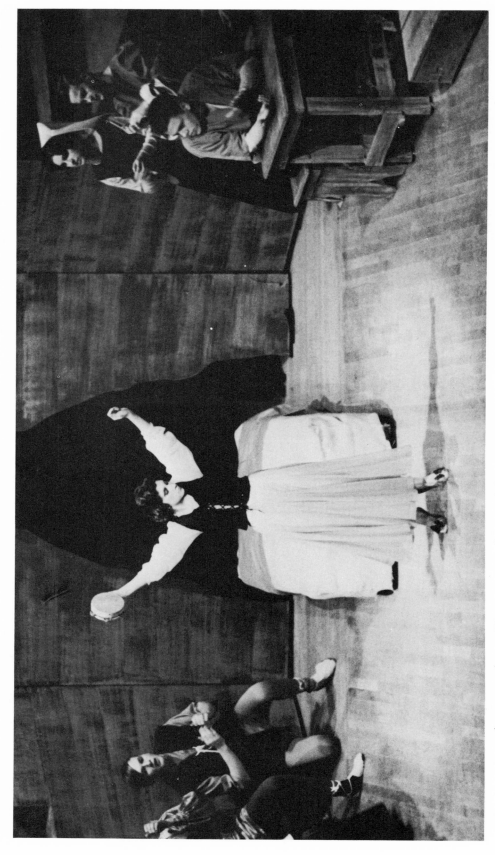

A scene from Everyman directed by William J. Martin at Culver Military Academy, Culver, Indiana. A medieval classic like "Everyman" lends itself to many types of staging.

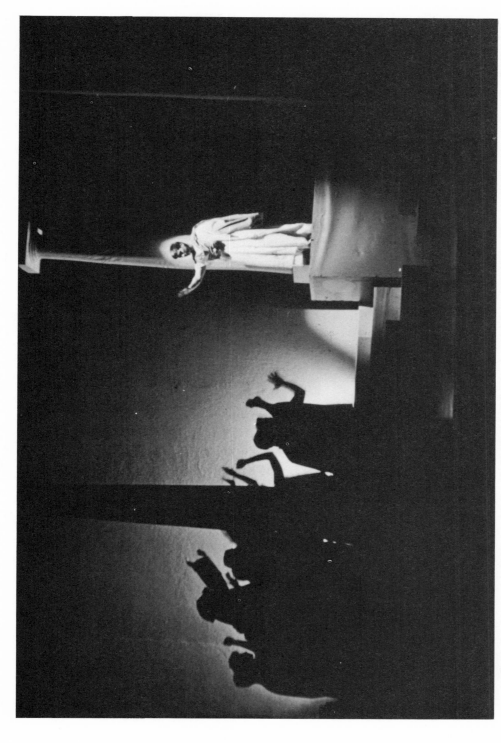

Brutus' oration from Julius Caesar directed by John S. Girault at Greeley (Colorado) Central High School. The crowd in silhouette looks larger and more dangerous than it would in full light.

A scene from The Miser directed by J. Cushman at the Shorewood (Wisconsin) High School. Molière wrote plays especially for his permanent company of professional actors. The plays need strong, vigorous action and believable characterization, not caricatures.

von Goethe, Richard Wagner, and the Duke of Saxe-Meiningen, all in Central Europe. Goethe trained a small company of actors to interpret completely and honestly the new nationalistic dramas that he and Johann von Schiller were writing. The company consisted of good actors, but they were under rigid discipline and were not allowed to embellish their roles. While most actors of the period walked through rehearsals mumbling their lines and saved their acting for an audience, Goethe planned every movement and vocal inflection and conducted complete rehearsals that were almost like performances.

The Duke of Saxe-Meiningen, who flourished in the latter half of the 19th century, built on Goethe's innovations but went even further. Before the first rehearsal he worked out on paper every detail of each of his productions: movement, grouping of characters, scenery, costumes, and properties. He was famous for his handling of crowd scenes. Actors were natural and seemingly spontaneous in their reactions. One reason for his success might be the high morale of his company. Actors would play leading roles one night and perform in mob scenes the next night. The Duke's great contribution was his meticulous attention to naturalistic detail. He might have been influenced by Charles Darwin and Émile Zola, whose writings and research emphasized the effect of environment on behavior and who laid the way for the naturalistic movement in the arts.

Richard Wagner, too, was unhappy with the discrepancy between author's intention and actor's performance. He wanted the production to be unified around a central concept. He wanted the scenery, lighting, actors, and costumes all to say one thing, not many individual things. He tied the actor's every movement and expression to whatever movement his music was expressing at a given moment. Wagner insisted that the performer's will become subservient to the music, and when he directed his own operas he achieved this goal. His grandsons have continued this tradition for today's audiences, but instead of Wagner's painted scenery they use gauzes and subtle lighting effects to achieve unity.

David Belasco, active in America at the end of the 19th and beginning of the 20th century, achieved a certain fame through his publicity campaigns for his leading ladies, but more for the naturalistic details of his settings. His sunsets were breathtaking. When he needed a cheap-looking bedroom he found one near Broadway and had its contents—even the wallpaper—removed to the stage. He cast carefully to type and turned unknown actors into stars overnight through his meticulous coaching.

Belasco was the last of the naturalistic directors, to be replaced by men such as Max Reinhardt and Konstantin Stanislavsky. The pendulum swung from emphasis on external details to inner truth. Gordon Craig and Adolphe Appia led the new movement in stagecraft with their theories and practice. They believed that the actors and scenery should evoke an atmosphere, not reproduce reality. Appia published his ideas on how to produce Wagner's operas in vast, suggestive settings bathed in subtle light, and Craig drew sketches for revolutionary non-realistic settings for Shakespeare and Ibsen.

Max Reinhardt introduced the theories of the new stagecraft to theatres in Europe and America, but his greatest contribution to the tradition of the director is in the *Regiebuch*. This was a series of notebooks he brought to rehearsals containing detailed notes on the production. Wide margins on either side of the play script allowed space for notes on characterization, properties, business, movement, grouping, lighting cues, sound cues, processionals, etc. Reinhardt visualized every phase of production before the first rehearsal; he achieved an impressive unity of effect because every detail was the product of a single mind. Reinhardt virtually hypnotized his actors into producing the effects he wanted. He never hesitated to show by voice or pantomime exactly what he expected from each actor. He left nothing to chance. His productions, whether intimate operas or spectacles, were artistically complete and based always on a unifying concept.

Stanislavsky, on the other hand, spent his life searching for the truth in acting rather than surface spectacle. He trained his actors meticulously in speech and bearing, and helped them develop their imaginations. He always went back to nature and life for his examples, because the theatre in Russia had become cliché-ridden. There was no ensemble acting, no interplay, no ultimate honesty, only trivial imitation of outworn habits. Stanislavisky changed all that by insisting that everything on the stage be lifelike, realistic, and enlarged by the actor's creative imagination. The actor learned to relate every action required by the play to some experience in his own life and thus give a new validity to all that happened on the stage. It is true that Stanislavsky misinterpreted Anton Chekhov's great comedies by treating them as tragedies, but in the process the actors learned to make the tiniest realistic detail significant. He also developed an ever-changing system of acting and directing that has profoundly influenced the theatre of the Western world. Actors are now encouraged to make the character their own by analyzing his motivations, after studying the playwright's intentions, and relating the character's experiences to those of the actor. This method is perfect for the subjective plays of Chekhov and Tennessee Williams, but if it is not well understood it does not train the actor for Shakespeare or the Greek masters.

Bernard Shaw should be mentioned in this survey of directors; he was the last great author-director of modern times, excepting of course Charlie Chaplin in Hollywood. As Shaw wrote his plays he included detailed stage directions for the actors and even indicated how lines should be read. He included this information partly for the benefit of readers who bought his plays in book form. Before Shaw, most contemporary plays were not made available to the public. Shaw read his plays aloud at the first rehearsal, indicating where audience reactions might come. During subsequent rehearsals he showed the actors how to execute business and movement and helped them speak his brilliant lines distinctly. His stage directions are still appropriate, because Shaw knew well the laws of attention. The Stanislavsky system would not be entirely satisfactory in a Shaw play because Shaw's emphasis is on ideas rather than on plot and characterization; his plays are cerebral rather than physical.

However, a contemporary director such as the famous and versatile Tyrone Guthrie is able to select techniques from preceding directors and invent others of his own as the situation requires. He is a master of theatre techniques and knows the value of dramatic pauses and sharp contrasts; of loud and soft, fast and slow, sentiment and farce; he knows the importance of masks, and the place of ritual in the theatre experience. Guthrie is a master in understanding actors and in developing a team to

George Schaefer coaches Genevieve Bujold in a scene from Saint Joan for NBC-TV Hallmark Hall of Fame.

produce a show. He is able to explain precisely to actors and designers the effects he wants, and he has the patience and enthusiasm to sit through long rehearsals until he gets what he wants. Always in the back of his mind is a strong picture of the impact he wants the play to create, and, with his capacity for total commitment, he does not rest until he achieves his goal. His plays are theatrical, dramatic, and full of surprises whether they are Shakespearean, Greek, musicals, modern farces, or serious plays. Always, the audience knows that it is attending an event, that it is present at an occasion.

Guthrie calls himself an audience of one, and as he watches a rehearsal he anticipates audience response by molding it. The confidence he builds up between himself and his actors spills over from the stage and engulfs the audience. Of course, he selects the best actors available for his plays and then trusts them to produce a believable characterization. But the extras, the soldiers and servants as well as the leading players, catch the spirit of the play from Guthrie's direction, so that no matter where you look during a performance, everyone on stage is concentrated on the same thing at every moment.

In this era of alienation, Guthrie can unite a group of spectators into a single unit by his mastery of theatre techniques. He knows how to seize attention, hold it, and direct it to whatever is important at the moment, be it a word or a gesture. This is the stuff of great theatre.

George Schaefer, successful director-producer of the Hallmark television plays, is another expert in stimulating audiences and actors. He studies every TV script carefully and decides what point he wants to make with each scene. He then decides how to achieve the point: by close-up, by grouping of the actors, by costume or vocal accent, by varying the tempo, by changing the vocal volume, or by music. He determines what he wants the audience to know or feel at the end of each scene and directs every effort of actors and production crew to that single effect. He, too, inspires confidence in his actors because he knows his goal before rehearsals start. Without prescribing precisely what his actors should do, he guides them into the kind of performance he wants by his calm, confident suggestions and hints. He keeps his actors comfortable, both physically and mentally, and makes each rehearsal a positive step toward the goal of performance.

Elia Kazan, famous for his directing of Tennessee Williams' plays and several motion pictures, gets superb performances from his actors first by casting strictly to type and then by conferring with his leading actors almost as a psychiatrist would. He forces his actors to penetrate deep into their subjective selves so that when they must cry out in anguish in the play, the cry comes from recalling a painful experience in their personal lives. He, too, knows the values of sudden contrasts in tempo—always justified, of course—the place of honest sentiment in the theatre, and the positive contributions an inspired scene designer can make to a production. He likes to work closely with the playwright before rehearsals begin, so that he understands every situation and every character. Kazan's intense and exciting style is so pronounced that his work has been advertised as "a Kazan production," taking precedence over the author.

Joshua Logan, best known for his direction of *South Pacific* and several William Inge plays, likes to work closely with his playwrights to be sure he understands every subtlety of the play. He does not hesitate to suggest changes that will make the play more effective theatrically. Although he has a master plan in mind before he comes to rehearsal, he likes to trust the inspiration of the moment, and he gives his actors freedom to experiment. He works on a scene from many different approaches until he finds the best way to perform it. One of his contributions to Broadway professionalism is the method he developed to lead from speech into song, as described in *Directing the Play,* edited by Toby Cole and Helen Krich Chinoy. The following paragraph is reprinted by permission of the publishers, The Bobbs-Merrill Company, Inc.

A song is about to start. Perhaps the author will have to write a little more of a scene before the song begins to establish the feeling of the scene. The actor and director heighten the emotion of a scene by performance. At the moment the apt emotional state is reached, the orchestra starts playing quietly under the dialogue to underline the emotional state. Just before the actual beginning of the song, perhaps the actor's voice can rise in emotion until, still speaking, this tone is colored to resemble singing. When he actually sings there should be a feeling that there is nothing left to do but sing. The song is simply a high moment in the story, never a departure from it.

Peter Brook directs successfully in England and America and is equally at home with *King Lear* or *Marat/Sade*. He stresses the contemporary note of shock and violence in his productions and soft-pedals any appeals to sentiment. His plays are full of strong positive action and theatrical effects. They are not subtle but hammer home their points with repetition and volume. The audience never forgets the experience. Brook's handling of a script is a kind of trademark and assures the audience it will be enthralled and alienated at the same time.

To conclude this prologue on directing and on specific directors, we shall catalogue briefly four general types of directors. It is true that each director develops his own style or manner of directing, but a review of the general types might be helpful.

First is the director who is not prepared, either because of heavy class work and committee obligations or because he does not know what preparation is needed. He comes to rehearsal and keeps his head in the playbook, literally following every suggestion offered in the script. He does not create anything new or interpret the script in theatrical terms. He sits at the edge of the stage and acts as a prompter and traffic cop. He is of little help to the actors, and he betrays his obligation to the audience.

Second comes the director who is over-prepared. He knows the play so well, is in such a hurry, and is so positive in his ideas that he acts out every role and insists that he be imitated. This method may be necessary with an occasional actor, but surely the whole cast cannot be unsuited to the material. If such a thing happens, the play was chosen without regard to the available actors. The imitation method is sometimes used by famous directors, but it leads to a performance without spark or spontaneity. Every actor acts like every other one because each is imitating the director. This autocratic system gives some directors a false sense of power, but it takes all the value and pleasure out of educational theatre.

Third is the specialist who is superb with one type of production: tragedy, melodrama, farce, comedy, serious play, or musical. He tends to select the same kind of play each season and justifies his choice by saying it is "what the audience wants." Specialization is necessary for Broadway, where directors are typed as actors are, but one of the advantages of educational theatre is that the director can grow in his career. He can select a play from an enormous collection and stretch himself as he meets the challenge of what seems at first impossibly difficult. He soon finds that the better the play, the more stimulating it is, and he can acquire a versatility the specialist will never enjoy.

Last is the generalist who is able to analyze all types of plays, who can discover the intentions of the author whoever he may be, who can communicate with actors, who knows theatre techniques and understands the needs of audiences. Ideally, he knows what is happening in the other arts and in daily life so that his productions are contemporary in every sense. However, he does not bludgeon his audience with accents that overemphasize relevancy for today in the classics. He lets audiences discover parallels for themselves. He chooses plays for his available actors and for the artistic progress of his own career. In short, the theatre educator is an alert person, a sensitive teacher, and an imaginative, creative theatrician.

Chapter I

CHOOSING A PLAY

Since putting on a play takes much energy, enthusiasm, and time, it is important to choose a good play in order to make the investment worthwhile. If a play is weak, every rehearsal is dull and audience reaction is minimal. As we use only good examples to teach music, English, and other subjects, so we should use only good plays when we teach the theatre experience.

It helps to have a rationale or philosophy as a guide in choosing plays. Sometimes tradition forces a rationale on us, but ideally it should grow out of the temperament of the director, the qualifications of the actors and backstage workers, and the appetite of the community. As a matter of fact, a good play like any other work of art is sufficient unto itself. If it brings pleasure or insight, it needs no other justification. Nevertheless, some students, parents, and administrators fail to grasp this point, and the director should have reasons at hand to justify the selection of a particular play.

There are at least six foundation stones that can provide, singly or in combination, a basis for selecting plays. First is the special opportunity *to supplement the education of cast, crew, and audience through vicarious experiences.* Shows such as *Our Town, Brigadoon, Inherit the Wind,* and *Our Hearts Were Young and Gay* deal with situations, characters, and environments that are far removed from routine daily experience and satisfy a natural curiosity about other people and other times. Discussion during rehearsals of any one of these plays, or of any good play for that matter, leads to an understanding of human motivation and often to startling discoveries about one's own character and capabilities. Putting on a play should always be a pleasant experience, but a good teacher-director can make the process a great learning device as well.

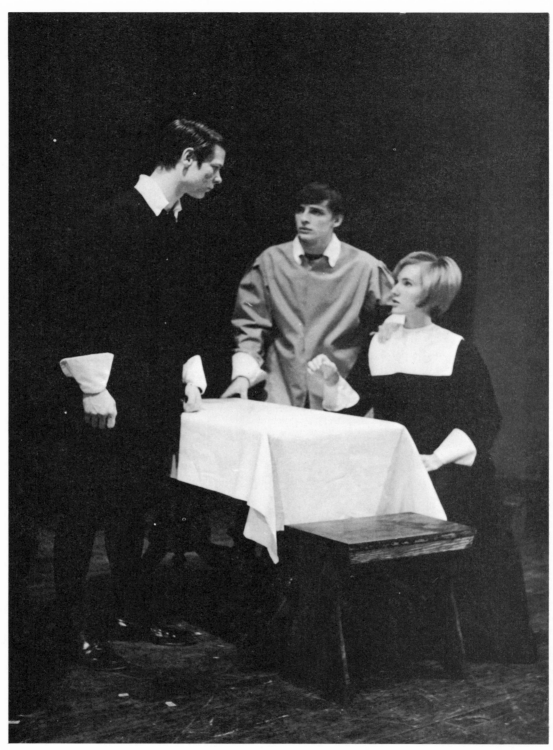

A scene from The Crucible *directed by David Giese at Mt. Pleasant (Iowa) High School. A scene built around a strong argument acts better if a table, bench or heavy chair separates the two fighters.*

Another reason for choosing a particular play is *to vitalize a curricular subject*. The play should not be something removed from the objectives of other aspects of school or community life. It should reinforce the general aims of education.

For example, the teacher-director could cooperate with his colleague and electrify the teaching of history by presenting plays such as *Abe Lincoln in Illinois, The Diary of Anne Frank, The Crucible, Sing Out Sweet Land, The Pursuit of Happiness*, or *Lawyer Lincoln*. The last-named play appears in the Appendix because it will be used throughout this book as illustrative material.

The guidance counselor or teacher of psychology would be interested in *Billy Liar, Bye Bye Birdie, The Miracle Worker*, or *The Music Man*. It is true that every good play has psychological overtones, but these four highlight certain aspects of psychology with exceptional clarity. This is not to say that, for example, the musicals *Bye Bye Birdie* and *The Music Man* are merely animated musical lectures on psychology, but the cast should be aware of the significance of what they are performing. *Billy Liar* is a vivid dramatization of a typical psychological phenomenon: the compulsion to daydream rather than face reality. Psychologists have always been interested in the theatre, and the interest of the guidance counselor is valuable and worth obtaining.

We cannot live effectively in today's world without knowing as much as we can about foreign cultures, and what better way exists than the theatre? *The Madwoman of Chaillot, Antigone, The Doctor in Spite of Himself, The King and I, Lady Precious Stream, The Marriage Proposal*, and *Benten the Thief*, a Japanese Kabuki melodrama, are examples of good plays that give tremendous insight into the culture of other nations. Such a play could be used as a springboard to arouse curiosity and initiate intensive study or as the climax of an extended period of study of a specific country.

The teacher of social studies should certainly be interested in plays that deal with family life, such as *The Happy Journey to Trenton and Camden, Life With Father, Sandbox, The Glass Menagerie, You Can't Take It With You, The Neighbors, This Property Is Condemned*, and *Sunrise at Campobello*. A sociolo-

A scene from The King and I directed by Julien R. Hughes at Leuzinger High School, Lawndale, California. This musical provides unusual insight into the culture of 19th-century Siam.

gist should also be interested in plays that throw a light on specific community problems, such as *The Hairy Ape, Bury the Dead, The Remarkable Incident at Carson's Corners, Plain and Fancy,* and *Finian's Rainbow.*

The English teacher would appreciate using plays as learning material if they fit into a course of study. Plays taken from literature, such as *The Barretts of Wimpole Street, Great Expectations, Tom Sawyer, Oliver!, Pride and Prejudice, I Remember Mama* or abridged versions of Shakespeare will, when produced properly, make the life of an English teacher a happier one.

The cooperation of other teachers on the faculty is always desirable. It adds to the educational significance of the play, sells tickets, and makes the production a school enterprise, not a private one.

The third foundation stone in our rationale is that working on a good play helps *to train the dramatic impulse,* which is present in everyone, but which without direction can turn into vandalism or fatal disinterest. Any urge as strong as the dramatic impulse must be nourished and directed by the arts, or it goes underground to reappear usually in a socially undesirable form. The dramatic impulse can be satisfied by working at a backstage job as well as by acting and directing. All the plays listed above will fulfill the needs of the dramatic urge, but certain plays, because of their theatricality, are more immediate in their appeal than others. The musicals *Carousel* and *Carnival* have all the qualities required for satisfying entertainment and are within the range of most amateurs. *The Typists, The Ugly Duckling, Aria da Capo* or a good play written for child audiences are examples of short plays with strong dramatic appeal. Among the long plays in this category are *The Fourposter, Charley's Aunt, Julius Caesar, Antigone,* and *Stardust.*

Another purpose of play production is *to develop self-reliance and cooperation.* Like a coach for an athletic team, the director of a play must develop a cohesive team, with each member subordinate to the chief purpose, which is to project an interpretation of life in dramatic form. There are no stars or leads in educational theatre, only members of a team. Self-reliance is acquired by actors and crew in the same way that ball players acquire it: They are trained so well by a director or coach that at game time they can play without having the coach on the field. The students should be able to put on a performance with the director sitting in the audience, in a more or less relaxed attitude. All plays depend on teamwork, but some are especially dependent on close interrelation between the actors. The husband-wife scenes from *Macbeth* fall into this category, as do *Little Women, In the Zone, Arsenic and Old Lace, The Grass Harp, Green Grow the Lilacs,* and a play for junior high actors called *The Clown Who Ran Away.*

By careful training the director can instill an amazing degree of self-reliance in students during the process of rehearsal and performance. The students should grow more independent as rehearsals proceed so that the director, if necessary, can be absent from the performance. Actually, part of the pleasure in directing comes from watching students develop strong self-discipline and self-reliance.

A fifth foundation stone in our rationale is the sense of obligation *to continue the tradition of theatre as education* that began in the monastery schools of the medieval period. Acting in plays was a succesful way of teaching language, fluency, poise, vocal skills, and reasoning. Schools for choir boys in the Elizabethan period and later under Jesuit supervision used theatre training for the same objectives. Good teachers have used theatre tools in their work for generations, with or without official approval. More and more schools are giving curriculum status to courses in theatre as administrators begin to recognize the tremendous possibilities of a good drama program.

Among plays written originally for young students are *Gammer Gurton's Needle, Ralph Roister Doister,* and two plays by Bertholt Brecht, *He Who Says Yes,* and *He Who Says No.* The Pyramus and Thisbe scenes from *Midsummer Night's Dream* make a good project for beginning or advanced actors. *The Blind* by de Ghelderode can be done by young actors. Occasionally a student writes a play or sketch that says something in a unique way, and it is almost a duty for the instructor to put it on the stage.

A final reason for producing a play is *to balance the mechanizing effect* of TV and motion pictures. A person can watch television without paying much attention, but watching a play on the stage requires a certain degree of concentration, a rare

A scene from Oliver! directed by Bert Rose at Wilbur H. Lynch High School, Amsterdam, New York. Oliver! is an ambitious musical requiring concentrated effort from many people but the results are worth it.

attribute today. Then, too, a stage play gives the environment and the group status as part of the total picture. Even more important is the direct contact possible in musicals and in some plays between living actors and a living audience. *Oliver!* and *My Fair Lady* are musicals that depend for their effect on frequent contact between actors and audience. Some plays use the venerable theatrical convention of "asides," meaning remarks that are supposedly heard only by the audience. Examples are *Only an Orphan Girl, She Stoops to Conquer, The Skin of Our Teeth, The Importance of Being Earnest, The Romancers, The Tempest,* plays of Molière such as *The Would-Be Gentleman* and *The Precocious Young Ladies,* and some plays for children. Audiences usually enjoy the special cameraderie made possible by direct address, and actors like to break through the relatively modern tradition of the invisible fourth wall.

Some reasons for choosing plays are not valid. Some schools still follow the tradition of putting on a junior or senior class play, and the director has to look for a play with exactly enough roles so that everyone in the class gets a part. This is an unfortunate tradition, and no one should be handicapped by this factor in his search for a good play. Another reason sometimes given is that a play will "enrich their minds." This justification is too vague to be of any value. The teacher should have a clear and definite reason for selecting a specific play, based on the factors listed in this chapter: to supplement the students' education through vicarious experiences; to vitalize a curricular subject; to train the dramatic impulse; to develop self-reliance and ability to cooperate; to continue the tradition of theatre as education; and to balance the effect of mechanizing entertainment media. When it is a good choice, the task of preparing the play is much easier and the results are more satisfactory for everyone involved.

The director of a civic group, like the teacher, should have a philosophy of play selection, and it can grow out of the principles explained in this chapter. People join an amateur group because they want some pleasant recreation, so the play or musical should meet that need. But they can grow in self-knowledge and in knowledge of other people and other cultures if the director uses the opportunities of the play to add to the education of his company.

Part of the audience at a play for children. The seats are on 7" terraces so that everyone has a good view of the stage. The theatre is small (172 seats), the acoustics are excellent, and the actors do not have to shout.

Children should be allowed to sit where they wish and not under the watchful eye of a teacher. They should feel free to shout and laugh and warn the actors and in general get thoroughly involved. A well-written play has moments of strong physical action and high excitement, alternating with moments of quiet and beauty. A good cast, well directed, can lead the audience through these moments successfully.

The audience should leave popcorn and candy bars at the door. This is not a movie theatre, but a community experience, and noisy cellophane wrappers or cracking gum can disturb the concentration of an audience. Television conditions children to expect frequent breaks in their concentration for commercials, but in the theatre the concentration is sustained. In order not to overstimulate the children or strain their ability to concentrate, the play should be no longer than 75 minutes, with very short intermissions.

If the community group wants to perform a civic service it can choose a play for children and use adults and teen-agers in the cast. It can tour elementary schools or take children by bus to a central theatre. Plays for children require more imagination and ingenuity in the design, more skill and vigor in the acting, more ability in the directing, and more time for rehearsal than a typical nonroyalty, three-act play with its unbelievable plot and stock characters. Whether the play is a classic like *Cinderella* or a modern fable like *Reynard the Fox,* the characterizations offer genuine challenge to young actors. There is no trouble in filling the theatre as often as necessary to accommodate the children in any community, and, best of all, an audience of children is quick to demonstrate approval or disapproval. This kind of audience is the best possible teacher for the actors and production staff. The sense of delight and desire to be entertained that children bring to the theatre is inspiring and demanding at the same time. Children cannot be satisfied by anything second rate. A cast and production staff soon learn that they must earn the respect of children and that once it is acquired they can provide a fascinating journey of exploration and discovery.

Sometimes it is difficult to persuade a group of students or civic members to attempt their first play for children, but after their first success they will want to do at least one a year. Touring a children's play is an excellent way to meet a community obligation, and it helps to make cast and crew responsible and independent individuals.

A play for children often encourages new reading habits in the audience. A director can enlist the aid of libraries and bookstores for displays centering around the play being produced. Teachers should be given study guides, reference material, and perhaps copies of the play so that they can prepare their classes in advance. The producing group, whether high school or civic, can follow up the performance with questionnaires or short reaction papers from which they can gain valuable information. Children can draw pictures of the characters or moments they remember best. This feedback from the audience will be flattering and astonishing. It will provide new information for everyone connected with the production.

In many communities a children's play series has been so successful that the producing group is able to finance the rest of the program with the surplus funds from the series.

Another factor that could determine the choice of play is that the group wants to perform in local hospitals and retirement homes. The need for entertainment in this field is tremendous, and the experience gained from touring to many kinds of audiences is always valuable to actors and directors.

Or the group could do plays from the series, "Plays for Living," which were written to provoke discussions on family and social problems by adult groups. These need to be acted very well, because they are thesis plays and the characters have to be fleshed out. They require very little scenery, usually only a table and chair, and they call for small casts. A discussion guide comes with each set of plays. It is surprising how much an audience can gain personally from discussions after the play, in which personal problems are probed in terms of the characters and situations. A group could acquire a powerful reputation by presenting these plays. The players could become a necessary part of the cultural program of the community, and theatre would lose any connotation of being an expendable frill.

The director might talk with managers of the local TV and radio stations and arrange for the group to present short plays, usually in the public domain, as part of the station's public-service obligations. If the group wants to televise a scene from its current production and it is a royalty play, the director must get permission from the publisher long in advance. Sufficient time should be allowed for rehearsal in the TV studio to accustom the cast to spaces that are smaller than usual.

Exposure on TV is an excellent way to be seen by a large audience. However, viewers today are so accustomed to highly polished shows prepared in Hollywood or New York that they will not tolerate anything amateurish. Therefore, we have to present scenes with our best actors and with the insurance of long rehearsal hours.

An ambitious civic theatre could prepare video tapes of scenes or entire plays to be used in schools, concentrating on plays being studied in literature classes. A good video tape of a well-produced play can give tremendous insight and appreciation to a group of students.

No matter how carefully a play has been chosen, some people are bound to be unhappy. Some actors will be disappointed, but if they have the right attitude to the theatre, their disappointment will not last long. An audience in despair because of the choice of play (not because of the production) is another matter. Too many disappointed audiences eventually produce empty houses. Some directors, however, cater too much to audience reaction. They follow literally the advice attributed variously to Colley Cibber or David Garrick:

> The dramas' rules the dramas' patrons give,
> And we who live to please must please to live.

Other directors deliberately ignore audience tastes. They like to shock a community simply for the sake of shocking. The theatre can be stimulating and exciting and still follow the dictates of good taste and common sense. At the same time, a director can slowly improve the taste of an audience so that it will accept thought-provoking, disturbing plays as well as light and entertaining ones.

The problem remains of what to do about self-appointed and extremely vocal critics.

One director in a medium-sized community chose *Ah, Wilderness!* for the Spring play. Two mothers wrote burning letters to the principal of the school after they had seen the play, calling it a piece of pornography and asking the principal to censor all future productions to protect the students from such "vulgarity."

The director could have exploded in anger, but instead she wrote a long letter to the mothers in which she calmly described O'Neill's international reputation and the popularity of the play for high-school groups in this country. She explained the enthusiasm of the students connected with the play and their close identification with the problems of the hero. She said, "The innocence of the teen-age hero and his tremendous triumph in remaining innocent in spite of the shoddiness of the adult world around him is an inspiration to the modern teen-age mind."

A worthy administrator or Board of Directors will always trust and support the staff. If the director is not sure of the possible effects of a certain play, he can have his superior read it before rehearsals begin and obtain support before, not after, the event.

Chapter II

INVENTORY OF SOURCES AND RESOURCES

Sometimes it is helpful to have a play selection committee to help the director make a choice. The committee members should have high theatre standards and know how to read a play so that it comes alive in their imagination. If necessary, the director can give the committee a choice of four or five plays. This method will prevent selection of an unsuitable play. A selection committee is a democratic device unless members vote for a play because it has juicy roles for themselves. In such a case, the director must emphasize the value of play production for many, not for just a few, and restate the criteria outlined in Chapter I: to enlarge the participant through vicarious experience; to vitalize the curriculum; to train the dramatic impulse; to develop self-reliance and ability to cooperate; to continue the tradition of theatre as education; to balance the effect of mechanical entertainment media; to provide a benefit for children; to promote discussion of a social problem; or to present a public service on TV or in institutions.

Certainly a knowledge of available physical resources will help to determine whether the production should be a play or a musical. A play depends for its effect on the power of the speaking voice. If the auditorium is too large—that is, over 750 capacity—beginning actors are handicapped by the lack of subtle vocal techniques. Even with amplification, a large auditorium presents difficulties for young actors. The size of the stage is also a determining factor. If it is tiny, a play with crowd scenes, such as *The Lottery,* will not be possible. *Dark of the Moon* and *Under Milkwood* need fairly large stages and good equipment to handle the lighting and scenic requirements. Sometimes a temporary apron or extension can be constructed in front of a small stage to accommodate the play. If *Peter Pan* is under consideration, the stage needs a good flying system and a grid above the acting area. Plays with one interior set, such as *The Curious Savage,* are better adapted to a small, shallow stage than plays requiring an exterior setting. Exteriors require a deep stage so that skies or landscapes can be lit properly.

The cooperation of the art department in designing and building the scenery and of the business education department in publicizing the play is often necessary and desirable. The director wins this cooperation when he convinces everyone concerned that he is not aiming for personal glory but for the glory of the theatre. "The play's the thing," not himself. He is interested in the growth of his actors and production team. He is interested in promoting and interpreting good plays. He is interested in the pleasure and satisfaction of the audience. When faculty members or town people are convinced of the motivation of the director, they will gladly cooperate. However, the director should ask for help early in the season, not at the last minute. The specialists in design and in publicity have their own activities and programs, but if they know what is wanted of them early in the season they can adjust their schedules accordingly.

If the director is considering a musical he needs, in addition, the full cooperation of the music department. Above all, he needs actors who can sing. *Cindy* and *Lute Song* are examples of current shows with incidental music in which the acting is of primary importance. *The King and I* requires very good acting in the leading roles, but for several smaller roles singing ability may take precedence. Another important requirement for a musical is a talented and dependable pianist who can teach vocal interpretation. Lacking such a person, the accompaniment for every song or dance should be recorded on tape to be played at every rehearsal. Of course, the pianist or full orchestra would be available for dress rehearsals and performances.

Sometimes the size or shape of the auditorium can be a factor in selecting a show. If there is a sunken orchestra pit, the chances of doing a successful musical are greater than if the orchestra is on the same level as the auditorium seats. For reasons of acoustics and visibility, the orchestra should be in a pit. Some theatres are rectangular and have many seats at the sides near the stage. These seats may be adequate when a speaker stands on the apron of the stage, but they are frustrating to an

Man of Destiny *in arena or center theatre directed by Paul Kozelka at Teachers College, Columbia University. With the audience sitting around the playing area, the actors do not come as close to each other as they would on a proscenium stage. More of the audience, therefore, will see more of the actors' faces than they would if the actors played at close range.*

audience when important scenes are played in upstage corners of the setting. For such theatres, it is wise either to rope off the poor seats or to design a very shallow setting, or both.

If no theatre is available, the potentials of arena theatre or center-stage techniques should be considered. Almost any large room, including gymnasiums, can be used in this technique. The audience sits around four sides of an oval or square acting space of at least 225 square feet. The actors can be on an elevated platform, or the audience can sit on bleachers. For some productions that need a suggestive or symbolic scenic background, the audience can be seated in a horseshoe arrangement on three sides of the acting area. Actors and audience alike seem to prefer a three-sided arena, because more of the actors' faces are visible to more of the audience than in true arena or center stage. The only other requirement for center staging is a good set of spotlights to light the actors and not the audience.

The ground plan for arena staging should have as much room as possible for actors to move about freely. Only essential pieces of furniture should be kept, and these should be placed if possible at the edges of the playing area. Furniture with low backs or backless seats such as benches and hassocks should be used.

The most effective plays for arena are comedies and farces because they involve almost constant movement. However, serious plays, children's plays, and musicals can also be successful. The advantage is that the actors do not have to shout to be heard.

The chief advantage to a producing group of having an arena of its own is that it is always available for rehearsals and performances and does not have to be shared with other groups. The room can be decorated at will and made to reflect various atmospheres, depending on the play. A group should be able to find unused space in a school, church, or community house that can be transformed into an arena theatre.

Before choosing a play, it is wise to know what is available and from whom. It is necessary to know in advance whether the play is restricted or available and what the royalty terms are. A nonroyalty play, unless it be a classic and in the public domain, is usually poor theatre and poor education; it bores those who participate and those who see it and offers no stimulation to the director. The royalty is a fair charge for an author's work, and it is extremely unethical and immoral to produce a play outside the classroom without making the proper arrangements.

It is best to read the play rather than a catalogue description of it, and there are many ways to obtain copies of good plays. The drama or extension departments of some state universities circulate copies of plays to any group in the state for short intervals. Sometimes play-producing groups within a community or school system can exchange copies of plays. Or the

A scene from We All Ganged Up on Everett Tuttle directed by Thomas J. Fenaughty at Teachers College, Columbia University. Original plays are rewarding to work on because cast and audience come to the play with open minds. They have no preconceived ideas on how it was done before. Sometimes new plays need cutting or rewriting or additional scenes, all of which can be done with the author present if he is available. Most authors are cooperative and willing to work with the director and actors. If they are not cooperative, they should be barred from the rehearsal room.

The Boy With a Cart *as a staged reading directed by Paul Kozelka at Teachers College, Columbia University. Since there was a certain amount of movement in this production, the actors carried their books with them, even though they had virtually memorized the script. Since it was a reading, there was no need for authentic costumes or make-up. This kind of production takes less time to prepare than a fully staged one, and it is appropriate for plays such as Shaw's* Don Juan in Hell. *However, audiences in general prefer a full production with its spectacle and movement.*

school library can order plays for classes and the same books can be used during the play-selection process.

If original scripts are wanted, a notice in the community or city newspaper will bring a flood of plays, some of which may be worthy of production.

If physical resources and time are limited, the director should consider a staged reading. In this form of Reader's Theatre, actors sit on stools or stand at a reading desk and suggest their characterizations. They do not act them out fully. They should memorize their parts so that they are free to establish contact with their partners, but they keep the scripts before them. Poetic plays are well suited to this kind of performance, as are narrative plays that do not depend on physical action. Some of Bernard Shaw's idea plays lend themselves well to Reader's Theatre.

The quickest way to find a play is to study catalogues and publications of theatre organizations. A letter on official stationery will bring useful information from the following publications, groups, publishers, and bookstores.

1. The American Educational Theatre Association, Executive Office, John F. Kennedy Center for the Performing Arts, 726 Jackson Place, N.W., Washington, D.C. 20006. Extremely valuable information is published in the quarterly journal and in the newsletters of its three divisions: The Children's Theatre Conference, The Secondary School Conference, and The American Community Theatre Association.

2. The National Contemporary Theatre Conference, John F. Kennedy Center for the Performing Arts, 726 Jackson Place N.W. Washington, D.C. 20006. Known formerly as the National Catholic Theatre Conference, this organization supplies information of all kinds to producing groups and has a lending library of over 2000 plays.

3. The National Thespian Society, College Hill Station, Cincinnati, Ohio 45224. The Society publishes *Dramatics Magazine* eight times a year. It promotes better theatre in secondary schools through the magazine and such services as royalty adjustment.

4. Drama Book Shop, 150 West 52nd Street, New York, N.Y. 10019. This store welcomes visitors and readers. It handles the plays of all publishers.

5. Samuel French, Inc., 25 West 45th Street, New York, N.Y. 10036. French's is the largest publishing house of its kind in the country.

6. Dramatists Play Service, 440 Park Avenue South, New York, N.Y. 10016. The catalogue from this company is conveniently arranged for easy reference.

7. Baker's Plays, 100 Summer Street, Boston, Massachusetts 02110. Modern and classical plays are listed in this catalogue, as well as plays for special occasions.

8. Dramatic Publishing Co., 86 East Randolph Street, Chi-

cago, Illinois 60601. The catalogue lists plays from the professional theatre and many written especially for nonprofessional actors.

9. Evans Plays, 500 East 77th Street, New York, N.Y. 10021. Long and short plays written in England and the British Empire are listed in the Evans catalogue.

10. Theatre Arts Books, 333 Sixth Avenue, New York, N.Y. 10014. Unusual plays are listed by this firm.

11. David McKay Co., Inc., 750 Third Avenue, New York, N.Y. 10017. The small catalogue contains important and impressive play titles.

12. "Plays for Living," Family Service Association, 44 East 23rd St., New York, N.Y. 10010.

13. The Anchorage Press, Cloverlot, Anchorage, Kentucky 40223. The catalogue lists excellent plays for children, written here and abroad, for teen-age or adult casts.

14. The Coach House Press, 53 West Jackson Boulevard, Chicago, Illinois 60604. This publishing house provides long and short plays for assemblies for teen-age actors and young audiences.

15. Plays Inc., 8 Arlington Street, Boston, Massachusetts 02116; Eldridge Publishing Co., Franklin, Ohio 45005; and T. S. Denison & Co., Minneapolis, Minnesota. With a high degree of discrimination and patience, a teacher can find on occasion a worthwhile play in their publications.

16. Tams-Witmark Music Library Inc., 757 Third Avenue, New York, N.Y. 10017.

17. Music Theatre International, 119 West 57th Street, New York, N.Y. 10019.

18. Rodgers and Hammerstein Repertory, 120 East 56th Street, New York, N.Y. 10022.

Besides ordering direct from publishers or the Drama Book Shop, the director can find many plays, both long and short, among the paperbacks in a good bookstore. It is necessary to point out that even though a book appears in a paperback anthology, the rules on royalty still apply.

Now that the director or the group knows what plays or musicals are available, it is necessary to investigate the resources of

A scene between pedant and servant in the 18th-century farce The
Weathercock *directed by Paul Kozelka at Teachers College, Columbia
University. The servant stands down center so that actors are drawn close
to the audience; he is an audio-visual object for the pedant's lecture
on anatomy.*

*A good farce or comedy can give as much insight into human nature as
a serious play does. Each character is obsessed by a particular desire,
such as money, love, reputation, etc., and loses his sense of proportion as
he pursues his goal. He says and does things that are funny to the audience but not to himself, because he must take himself and his obsession
seriously or the audience will not respond.*

talent. A play needs actors, a stage manager, a technical crew for lights and scenery, a costume crew, a property crew, and a publicity and house management crew. A musical needs actors who can sing, an orchestra, a musical director, a choreographer, and the same crews, augmented, as needed by a play. A director who works with a drama group has an idea of what talent is available before tryouts are held, but he should never even imply that a play is already cast before tryouts begin. If the actors think a play is practically cast in advance, they will lose all enthusiasm. Furthermore, the director should keep his mind open for new talent that may show up at a tryout.

To get an idea of the degree of interest in a production, the director should call a general meeting, advertising the event and asking for backstage workers and actors. The meeting can be short. The director states that a play or musical will be chosen; he introduces the musical director, who is usually a member of the faculty, the choreographer, and, if possible, the adults in charge of scenery, costumes, and publicity. Then he passes out sheets of paper on which students write two or three preferences for participation, choosing among cast and one of the crews. It might save time if all the positions open were listed so that only the numbers 1, 2, 3, indicating preference, need be written in. In order to keep the spotlight on the importance of backstage work, it is preferable to list these positions first and follow with cast openings.

The meeting ends with several group improvisations that include everyone at some time, whether their interest is cast or crew. Improvisations are useful not only at this general tryout but at various stages during the rehearsal period. They can be loosely structured or tightly planned. Their value lies in the spontaneous reactions actors elicit from each other, in the sharp listening habits required to participate, and in the exercise of imagination that the actors experience. Two or three people may be given a cartoon and asked to build up to the scene shown. Or the director may outline a situation, such as a landlady interviewing a prospective tenant, robbers fighting over division of their loot, a mother and daughter preparing dinner for the daughter's suitor, a woman telephoning an obstinate client, a neighborhood group relaxing on a hot summer evening but end-

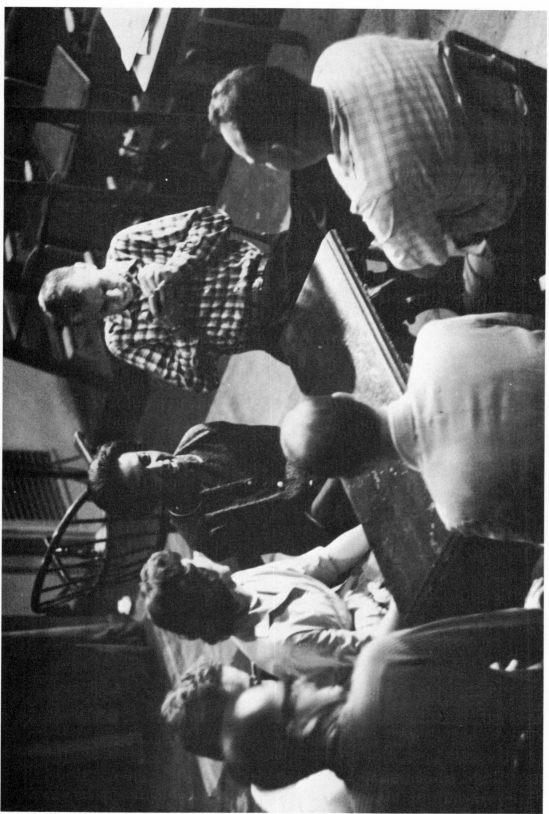

"Skull session" for a series of improvisations for a public production at Teachers College, Columbia University. Improvisations are valuable as a training tool but with experienced actors they can be developed into entertaining sketches or blackout scenes. They should be rehearsed enough to establish the beginning and end but not so much that they lose the feeling of spontaneity. Material comes from newspapers, cartoons, joke collections and TV and is hammered into usable form at rehearsals.

ing with an argument over a lost or stolen object. The director should invent conflict for the characters so that the scene can reach a climax. The improvisations should be timed so that they do not ramble beyond the point of no return. Ideas for improvisations can be drawn from sketches seen on TV. A good five-minute "improv" can be laid in a park, a zoo, a carnival, a store, or on a beach, or one can be taken from Viola Spolin's book *The Uses of Improvisation* (Northwestern University Press, 1963). The improvisations may reveal unexpected ability and imagination, but more important, they should be fun and appeal to the love of theatre that drew everyone to the meeting in the first place.

If the director knows what talent resources are available in his school or community, he can omit the general tryout and proceed directly to tryouts for a specific play. He can advertise the play or musical and make copies available in various locations so that candidates can become familiar with it. By choosing a show a season in advance he will have more time to plan and to make arrangements with the agent or publisher. Sometimes a play is restricted, meaning that it may not be performed in certain areas because of the possibility of a road company's passing through or because it is being considered for a motion picture or a TV special.

If the director has called a general tryout to learn what talent resources he has at his disposal, he is now ready to begin a fruitful search for the right play by reading catalogues and the plays themselves. He is also ready to draw up lists of crew members and a production calendar.

Concurrently, he can take stock of his own resources and strengthen them where they are weak. Presumably he is interested in the theatre and likes to work with people. He also has vast supplies of energy and patience. He can learn his craft by experience, but he can prepare himself for the first plunge in a number of ways. He can read books by or about directors such as Tyrone Guthrie, Stanislavsky, Harold Clurman, and Alexander Dean. He can listen to recordings of great plays, classical and modern, produced by The Theatre Recording Society, from which he can learn about timing, vocal range, characterization by voice alone, the effectiveness of vocal contrast in the

The famous recognition scene from "Anastasia" performed by Julie Harris and Lynne Fontanne for the NBC-TV Hallmark Hall of Fame production. Facial expressions and gestures are small and subtle for TV, and enlarged for the stage, but the actor's thought process is the same for either medium.

cast, the importance of picking up cues, and the need for contrasts in tempo. He should read the script as he listens to the record, and imagine actors entering, taking positions, executing business, and interacting with each other.

Much can be learned about the theatre by reading good books about actors, such as the one on Alfred Lunt and Lynn Fontanne called *Stagestruck,* by Maurice Zolotow, or the one on Sarah Bernhardt, *Madame Sarah,* by Cornelia Otis Skinner. These books and others describe the discipline and attention to detail typical of the great actor.

Motion pictures and television shows can be very informative to a perceptive neophyte. Notice what camera techniques the director uses for emphasis and for calling attention to a certain event, person, or object. Our job in the theatre is to hold attention and then shift it as the play demands. The director in TV and films uses music and extreme close-ups and montage effects that are not possible in the theatre. But we can learn other directing techniques such as grouping or picturization, the effect of levels (steps and platforms); the difference between movement directly toward or away from the camera (upstage, which is away from the camera or footlights, and downstage, which is toward the camera or footlights) and movement across the screen (from left to right stage); the effect of changes in tempo and in position; and building up to and away from minor and major climaxes. Such close observation of camera techniques may at first detract from your enjoyment of the plot, but eventually it develops a deeper appreciation of the art of motion pictures and TV.

There is now available to Educational TV stations a series of tapes of rehearsal scenes that can be very helpful to the director. The scenes are under the direction of Barry Boys, who has an excellent way of helping his actors to find the right interpretation and characterization. This series or a similar one on rehearsing can probably be obtained from the nearest ETV station for private or public screening.

Chapter III

PREPARING SCHEDULES

Let us assume that the play or musical has been chosen. The director can now proceed to the task of preparing work schedules. Only general outlines will be presented here; the subject of backstage management and publicity are covered in another book in this series.

Crews are an important part of the play production process for four reasons. First, so many tasks must be performed that no one person is capable of doing them all. Hence, the jobs must be divided up and crews appointed to do them. When you next see a movie or a TV show notice how many names appear on the credit lists; there are directors and supervisors for every aspect of the production, including hair dressing. Second, a system of working crews linked by good communications can be an important factor in maintaining morale. Third, many people who are drawn to the theatre either do not like to act or are afraid to try, but they can contribute to the success of the play by working in relative anonymity on a crew. The final reason is to insure that all the work is done in time for the dress rehearsal. A well-organized system of backstage crews is the best insurance a director can acquire.

From the names secured at the open tryout the director can choose an experienced crew head, an assistant head, and three to ten students for each crew. The crew head should know the rudiments of the task to be done, be a good organizer, and have the respect and loyalty of his crew. The assistant head is a trainee who is being groomed for the job of crew head for the next show. The size of the crew depends on the scope of the job to be done before dress rehearsal. The important thing to remember is to use everyone who expressed an interest at the open meeting.

To be appointed are crews (1) to make and handle scenery;

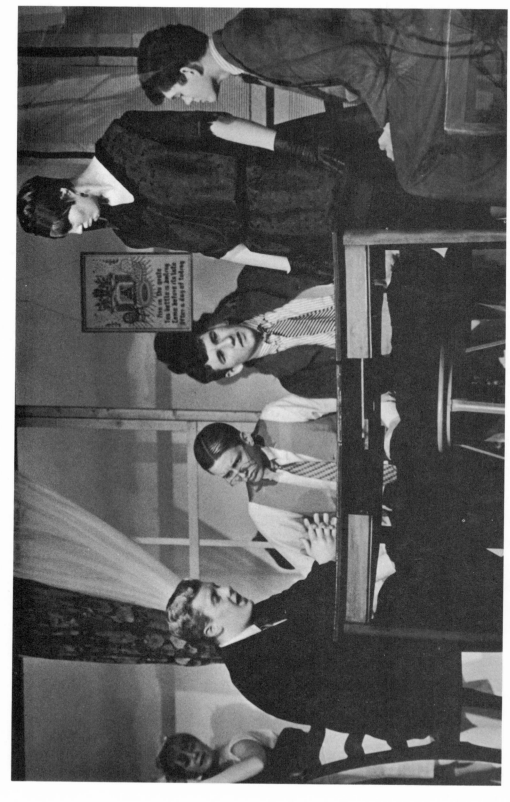

A scene from Molly Morgan adapted from a story by John Steinbeck and directed by Mary Kessler at The Principia, St. Louis, Missouri. Middle-age characters are difficult to portray with teen-age actors but close observation, imitation and make-up can all convey believability.

(2) to hang and run the lights; (3) to make costumes; (4) to handle makeup; (5) to take care of publicity; and (6) to manage the audience. Sometimes the crews are supervised by a faculty member, sometimes not. This depends on the abilities of the crew head and the crew itself.

The director should meet frequently with the crew heads individually or as a group to check on progress and to guarantee communications.

Other appointments to be made are assistants to the director, the choreographer, and the director of music. These student assistants can enter changes in the prompt script, conduct rehearsals, and help to keep lines of communication open. Student assistants are important people, not flunkeys. They should have a genuine feeling of responsibility for the success of the production. They should know the objectives of the crew head to whom they are assigned, and they should understand the director's conception of his goal. They should attend production meetings at which the director and heads discuss problems, and they should be given specific responsibilities and deadlines. Problems or questions to be resolved should go from crew member to assistant to crew head to director.

Crew heads and their assistants can be trained in the technique of micro-teaching; that is, instructing three or four persons at one time instead of a large group. The director's assistant, for example, can handle rehearsals of three or four actors very satisfactorily, once he understands the director's goals. He can even be entrusted with details of interpretation. Sometimes actors can rehearse by themselves, but usually they prefer having someone to watch who can give suggestions for improvement. The type of small group work implied in micro-teaching is one of the most valuable by-products of the entire production process.

Next comes the job of preparing production schedules, lists of deadlines by which various parts of the production must be completed, including performance dates. Educationally, it is better to have two weekends of performances rather than a continuous schedule. Young actors become over-excited and exhausted if they have to give a series of dress rehearsals followed by four or five consecutive performances. With a two-weekend schedule, the

A scene from Noah *directed by Bradford White at Memphis (Tennessee) State University. The ramp and ark structure provide excellent opportunities for emphasizing certain actors through triangular composition. A structure such as this must be available to actors early in the rehearsal schedule.*

members of the cast can recoup their energy and incorporate into the production what they have learned from the audience reaction.

Before selecting performance dates, consult the school calendar to avoid a conflict with a big game or dance. The community calendar, too, should be checked to avoid unnecessary competition. These considerations are less important if the play is designed for children, since they are not usually involved in high-school or community events.

When the production dates are chosen, they should be entered in the school calendar. In large communities it is probably wise to choose performance weekends a year in advance so that everyone can plan accordingly.

On the production schedule, the director should list deadlines for the crews responsible for props, costumes, scenery, lights and sound, and publicity. Working props should be ready three weeks before the first dress rehearsal, real props one week before. Costumes should be ready several days before the first dress rehearsal; but for big or unusual costume plays, rehearsal skirts for the girls and rehearsal jackets or breeches for the men should be ready three weeks before the first dress rehearsal. The lighting and sound crews should know when preliminary plans are due and when the technical and dress rehearsals are scheduled. The publicity crew should know the full production calendar so that they can draw up their own schedule of publicity releases.

Deadlines for the scenery crew should include dates for submitting designs, completing construction, and painting and installing scenery. For example, actors need to rehearse as early as possible on structures such as the tree platform in *The Grass Harp*. They must get used to the steps leading up to the platform and the platform itself. If they waited until dress rehearsal, there would not be time to adjust lines or business to the new situation. Actors must negotiate stairways and platforms smoothly and with the proper timing and this comes only after repeated practice with them. In the case of the tree platform, the skeleton frame should be ready for the actors as soon as they begin to block out the movements. If they cannot work on the stage, they should rehearse in the shop where the tree and platform are being constructed.

Next the director should draw up a tentative rehearsal schedule, specifying the times for beginning and ending each rehearsal, the run-through rehearsals when the entire cast is needed, the rehearsals for only specific characters, the technical rehearsal, and the dress rehearsals. Many open spaces should be provided in the schedule to allow for special rehearsals of groups or individuals as the need arises. It is desirable to hold all rehearsals in the theatre where the performance is to take place. The swimming team practices in a pool, not a classroom; and a cast should rehearse in an auditorium, for much the same reasons. Actors must learn to project voices and characterizations, which cannot be done in a small room. When the auditorium can be used only for dress rehearsals and performances, it should be reserved as soon as dates are scheduled. For a full-length play or musical three weekends are necessary, one for dress rehearsals and two for performances.

A musical needs at least two rehearsal rooms, one with a piano for practicing the songs and another for rehearsing the spoken portions. A small room is satisfactory when the play is long and has several scenes involving only two or three actors. Such a room can be used for discussing the author's intentions, motivations, and character relationships. As a general rule, however, it is uncomfortable and dangerous for actors to work in cramped quarters. Exceptions are rehearsals devoted to blocking (planning patterns of movement) and to love scenes, which often can be worked out more easily in a living room without onlookers than in a large hall.

A short play such as *Lawyer Lincoln* involves a shorter rehearsal and production schedule, but all the stages of the long schedule should be included. If the play is intended for an assembly program the reservation of the auditorium is still recommended.

It is not practicable to include a sample schedule, because conditions differ in each community. In some cases rehearsals can be held at night or on weekends; in others they must be held during school hours. A good rehearsal with one or two actors on lines or characterization can be squeezed into a free period, a lunch period, or before the school day begins. With adult actors, rehearsals should be work sessions, not times for socializing.

Rehearsals can be isolated to concentrate on movement, characterization, business, or interaction, but actors progress at such different rates that they may not all be ready to work on characterization, for example, at the same time. The only rehearsals with definite labels should be those at the beginning of the schedule to read the play, discuss it, and block out the big movements; the one by which lines should be learned cold; and the dress rehearsals and performances.

Copies of the schedule should be widely distributed. They should be given to administrators and members of the board of directors, if there is one; these persons in authority should be aware of the great amount of time that goes into the preparation of a show. The director needs all the cooperation and understanding he can get from administrators, and he must take all opportunities to make them realize the cultural and educational growth that occurs during rehearsal and performance. Educators have persuaded the powers that be of the need for official practice time for athletes and musicians, but theatre directors have not been so successful.

However, with all the current enthusiasm for living theatre being shown by government, foundations, and local groups, the task of demonstrating the values of theatre is becoming easier. Some schools enjoy performances of classics by professional companies, but most student bodies learn more and gain more enrichment by producing their own plays at as high a level of excellence as possible.

The next step in the production process is to draw up a tentative budget to enable the director to demonstrate how much money he needs to put on the show. This budget and the production schedule are effective evidence that the director is an organized planner and not flighty and impetuous.

Items to be included in the budget include royalty charges and the cost of buying or renting the play or musical work. The costs for scenery, costumes, and makeup can be estimated by the crew heads. The approximate cost of tickets and posters can be determined by telephoning several printing concerns. The budget should be approved by the principal or the treasurer or controller, and every effort should be made to stay within the figure agreed upon.

It is difficult to estimate box-office receipts on a first show. For a play, attendance might be 60 percent of capacity on Friday evening and 80 to 90 percent on Saturday. Musicals attract larger audiences, so 90 percent of capacity can be expected for each performance. Children's plays, usually given in the afternoon or Saturday morning with a family show on one evening, always attract large audiences; but since the ticket price is lower than for a play or musical, the receipts are correspondingly lower. Experience in the community will make it possible to judge box-office receipts with reasonable accuracy. Another source of income is program advertising; this subject, like ticket selling, is covered in another book in the Theatre Student series.

With the production schedule and the budget prepared, the director is ready to announce the play or musical chosen. The school newspaper, the public-address system, or the community newspaper can be used to publicize the name of the production and the date of the first tryout for roles. Before tryouts are held, however, the director needs to spend time analyzing the play, so that he can come to tryouts and the first rehearsal with definite ideas in mind. The process of analysis will be explained in the next chapter.

Chapter IV

ANALYZING THE PLAY

In this chapter we shall describe the director's most important obligation, that of play analysis, and outline several approaches to this task. The director must analyze the play thoroughly before calling a cast together. Only he can decide how the play is to be interpreted. When he has made his preliminary decisions, it is easy to cast the play and to settle problems that come up during rehearsal.

Plays may fail for many reasons: weak plot, poor dialogue, bad acting, inadequate lighting or scenery, poor acoustics, insufficient rehearsal, and occasionally an unappreciative audience. But the most common reason is misinterpretation by the director.

In one producton of *Aria da Capo,* the fantasy-like fable was performed as a heavy, ponderous, slow tragedy, as though every line had profound significance. The actors moved around slowly, put in long pauses, and in general failed to capture the make-believe quality written into the play.

Lawyer Lincoln can easily be misinterpreted. Lincoln can be portrayed as a serious Solomon figure passing judgment, Sis can be played as a fussy busybody, Nate as an ignorant country bumpkin, and the townswomen can become caricatures. The play thus could be turned into a boring sermon, and an audience would be justified in walking out.

The three approaches to play analysis are the intellectual, the intuitive, and the dramaturgical, and they will be considered in that order.

Questions to be answered in the intellectual analysis are: Why did the author write the play? Is the purpose imaginative entertainment as in *Visit to a Small Planet?* Is it entertainment and insight as in *Teahouse of the August Moon?* Is it a revelation of incredible courage as in *Diary of Anne Frank?* Is it a semific-

Peter Ustinov as Socrates and Geraldine Page as his wife in Barefoot in Athens for the NBC-TV Hallmark Hall of Fame production. The conflicts in this play are not wide and boisterous but small and deep.

tional episode in the life of a historical figure as in *Lawyer Lincoln?*

Some authors such as Bernard Shaw, William Saroyan, Thornton Wilder, Maxwell Anderson, and Eugene Ionesco write essays for their plays to explain the purpose. Others, including Edward Albee and Tennessee Williams, expect the director to discover the purpose as he studies the play. Sometimes a clue to the intention or meaning lies in the title, as in *The Happy Journey from Camden to Trenton* or *Our Town*. Notice that *Lawyer Lincoln* is not called *President Lincoln* or *The Martyred President* or *Lincoln as Head of a Family*. The play concerns Lincoln before he became a national figure burdened by problems of state; hence his humanity, naturalness, and humor are emphasized. Given the nature of a play as a condensed form of narrative, the authors are able to bring together many anecdotes and examples of Lincoln's wisdom and concentrate them into one short scene.

After deciding what the author's intention might be, the director next studies the play to discover its dramatic and theatrical values. What are the events or moments that make it a theatrical experience rather than a short story? In every play the conflict between characters or between characters and events is always a strong dramatic value. In *Anne Frank* suspense and characterization are important, whereas in *Teahouse* spectacle and situation are dominant values. In *Lawyer Lincoln* characterization is important, and so is the suspense connected with the marriage proposal. The battle of wits between Lincoln and the Judge is a theatrical value, as is the square dance with its movement and festivity. The young lovers and the townspeople have high comic value, but of course the actors play the roles seriously. The chorus singing offstage during the love scene provides a sentimental value. There is irony in Lincoln's serving as a romantic go-between, and humor in his acting unconsciously like a lawyer in the proposal scene. All these dramatic values and others must be discovered, analyzed, and then projected from the stage in such a way that the audience will appreciate them.

Now comes the director's decision on the theme or moral of the play as he sees it. The theme can be a quotation from the play or a sentence constructed by the director. In either case it will set the general tone or mood of the play and have a subtle effect on the audience. Different directors will select different themes for the same play. For *Lawyer Lincoln,* the theme could be "Every problem carries a solution within it," or "Don't make hasty conclusions," or "Young lovers need the wisdom of age to overcome difficulties," or "Nothing is more important than the happiness of young people." One young director, overly zealous from his psychology courses, decided that the theme for Wilder's *Happy Journey* centered on a neurotic, possessive mother's domination of her family during an automobile trip. He had not sensed the tone of the play, and he considered the title a sarcastic reference. It is desirable to establish a theme early, because most of the decisions a director has to make are affected by it consciously or subconsciously.

After selecting a theme, the director should divide the play into acting units, to be sure that the audience understands each part of the play as it progresses. An acting unit is a small or large section of the play that achieves a specific objective. Such a division emphasizes the high points of the play and enables the director to guard against monotony. It also can help him draw up a rehearsal schedule by showing which actors are needed for each part of the play.

The first unit of a play is usually expository, giving the audience important information about who, what, when, where, and why. In *Lawyer Lincoln* unit one is the opening scene between Sis and Nate, in which we discover their character relationship and that Nate is in love. Unit two still revolves around Sis and introduces Lincoln, Judge Davis, and Lawyer Craig. It contains some exposition concerning the problem of finding a jury for the coming session, but the main point is to present the wager between the three men about Lincoln's wasting of time. Two important events happen in unit three: Lincoln persuades Nate to serve on the jury, and the Judge convinces Nate that he may not talk to anyone since he has become a juror. Unit four is a short, pleasant interlude in which several townswomen arrive for a Harmony session and try in vain to interest the Judge and Craig in joining them, and in unit five Keenie and Nate almost break up their relationship. In unit six Lincoln serves as mediator between the two young people. This is the longest unit in the play and requires careful acting by the three characters. The climax comes in unit seven when Nate breaks his silence with a shout to keep Lincoln from kissing Keenie. The plot is resolved when Lincoln receives the Judge's promise not to lecture him again. Unit eight is a pleasant denouement in the form of a lively square dance and song to celebrate Keenie's engagement.

This division of the play into acting units is organic rather than arbitrary. Of course, the director will work on the transitions between units so that one flows smoothly into the next.

The next major step in analyzing a play is to plot the major and minor crises. Even the lightest comedy has a number of critical moments when audience interest rises to a peak, and the director must stage these moments fully to do justice to the play and its dramatic progress. The major climax in our play is the moment when we hear the answer to the big question: Will Nate win Keenie? Nate explodes out of his silence and learns that he can talk freely until he enters a jury room. He kisses Keenie to settle the question.

At least five minor crises in the play contribute to its suspense and forward movement. These minor crises can be stated as questions:

Will Nate walk Keenie home?
Will Lincoln agree to a bargain with the Judge?
Will the Judge and Lawyer Craig sing with the ladies?
Will Nate break his promise and speak to Keenie?
Will Lincoln succeed as he proposes for Nate?

Having identified the crises in a play, the director keeps them in mind all through rehearsals so that they stay sharp, distinct, and recognizable, because actors tend to blunt the climaxes when they play them repeatedly. The actors should be made aware of the importance of these dramatic moments and taught how to project them through volume, intensity, pauses, movement, or other definite techniques.

The next step in analysis is to isolate the chief acting problems in the play. This process helps the director to understand the form or structure of the play and in addition gives him ideas on what qualities to look for during tryouts. Probably the major acting problem in any one-act play is how to establish the identity of a character quickly. The audience learns a lot about a character from his appearance and the way he moves and reacts, long before he says a word. It is important, therefore, to think about costume, bearing, and movement for each person and to experiment in rehearsals until the proper mode is achieved. Each character in *Lawyer Lincoln* should be identifiable as he or she walks or runs on stage. Does this mean typecasting? It certainly does. Sis should look and act like a woman of forty and Nate should look like a young man of twenty-one, whereas the Judge and Lawyer Craig should look and act like mature men.

Another acting problem in many plays is to make an essentially negative character such as Nate likable and interesting. A young man with a strong, vivid personality can be cast as Nate to overcome the character's passivity. He can be alert and dynamic in his scenes with Lincoln, and he can resist the temptation to be excessively bashful with Keenie. The man who plays Lincoln can keep him interesting by revealing more and more of his characteristics as the play progresses. Lincoln does not retain the same mood throughout the play. He should change visibly and audibly as often as the mood of the scene changes. Lincoln is neither a historical monument nor a law-giving Moses in this play, and he should react as a normal man to all the people and situations he meets. One of the problems connected with his character is how to keep the pace of the play alive and spirited and still establish his easy-going nature. The key to it lies in the alertness and speed with which Lincoln picks up his cues with a glance, a gesture, a smile, or a word.

Other acting problems concern Keenie, the townswomen, Nate, and the Judge. Keenie could become a mean, petty, spoiled child if overplayed. She should retain audience sympathy in all her scenes. Each of the townswomen should have a distinctive bearing, mental attitude, and manner of responding. Nate's long silence must be justified and made interesting by keeping his reactions sensitive, varied, and growing in intensity. The conflict between Lincoln and the Judge is serious but not bitter or vindictive. The Judge is determined to win the wager, but Lincoln is more interested in matching wits. Finally, the celebration dance offers a challenge because it must build in interest and involvement as it proceeds. The director can build interest by increasing the tempo and volume of the music so that the play ends on a high pitch in contrast to the relaxed opening. Other acting problems will arise depending on the cast, but they can all be solved within the general framework presented here.

A necessary and time-consuming part of the director's process of analysis is research. The director should be ready to help the cast with information about the author, the leading characters, and the period of the play in reference to setting, properties, costumes, and manners. Research on a particular play can be divided into units or topics and given to individual students or groups. It is necessary, of course, to obtain the cooperation of the library staff and other resource people in the community. For *Lawyer Lincoln,* for example, it would be helpful to know that Betty Smith's writings usually are robust, vigorous, and sentimental, and that she is interested in the motivations of characters, not in melodramatic excitement. The material on Lincoln is almost boundless and comes in many forms and for all levels of reading ability. Research on Lincoln for this play, especially with Carl Sandburg's books, might inspire a student to study all of Lincoln's life; or he might develop a lifelong interest in the period. We learn from historical sources that in 1849 Lincoln spent half the year as a new Congressman in Washington, and half the year traveling the Illinois judicial circuit. It is one of the circuit visits that the playwrights have expanded into an imaginative entertainment.

For this and other plays, the librarian can find books on costumes, architecture, and manners for a given period or place. She might have a recording of the play or one in a similar style to help students appreciate emotionally and sensually the drama they are producing. A biography of the author or of the leading figures if they are historical, as well as reports on the music, literature, and social and political life of the era, will make the play a living experience instead of a museum piece.

Another aspect of the intellectual analysis of the play is to count the number of lines (not speeches) of each character. This gives the director helpful information when he casts the play and draws up the rehearsal schedule. An actor who has trouble memorizing would not be given the role with the most lines. The characters with many lines should have many rehearsals. In

Lawyer Lincoln, for example, a reader gets the impression that Nate has few lines. An actual count reveals, surprisingly, that he has more lines than Keenie. Lincoln, of course, has the greatest number, Sis is second, and the Judge has as many as Nate.

Another step in the intellectual analysis of a play is to read it aloud in one sitting without an audience, except perhaps a pet dog or cat. This process gives the director a kinesthetic appreciation of the play. It shows him how the play rolls along and grows in complexity, it makes the small and large climaxes evident, and it reveals the extent of individualization the author has accomplished. The director also hears the different speech rhythms unique to each character in a good play and hears or feels the changing rhythmic pattern of the whole.

He should be able to predict fairly accurately where an audience might laugh during a comedy, and he can think about how he wants to handle the laughs. The first laugh response from an audience is an important one, and the director can decide where it should come. It could be triggered by a piece of business or a line of dialogue. In any case, the audience needs to know early in the play whether it is a serious work or a comedy, and they get their impressions from the attitudes and actions of the actors. Hence it is important that the director sense the tone of the play during the process of analysis, and one of the easiest ways to discover it is by hearing himself read it aloud.

A final step in the intellectual analysis of a play is to discover what each character does *in* the play and what he does *for* the play. This process helps the director keep the play alive, progressing, and clear. Draw a line down the center of a sheet of paper. In one column list the specific actions as they occur chronologically. In the second column explain the significance of each action. For example, in *Lawyer Lincoln,* Nate says to his mother, "No, Maw! Not Mr. Lincoln. Don't tell him nothin's wrong with me. Don't you dast!" His action is to jump up from the table. The significance of the action reveals Nate's attitude toward Lincoln. The audience gets the idea that Nate's problem is too personal to discuss outside the family, that he is unsophisticated, and that a crisis is brewing inside him.

So far, the director's analysis has consisted of verbal and log-

Emotional response to Lawyer Lincoln *by Bernard Maas.*

ical devices. A form of play analysis that requires intuitive thinking is the depiction of the director's impression of the play in what is known as an emotional response. This is a drawing with colored chalk, paints, Magic Marker, or crayons of the director's private, personal reaction to the play as a whole or to the climactic moment. It is abstract, not representational. Through color, line, and mass, it depicts an impression or mood, the protagonist's journey, or the general emotional flavor of the play. It is important and meaningful only to the director. For *Lawyer Lincoln* the emotional-response drawing might show all the figures in brightly colored symbols with a continuous line representing Lincoln touching and affecting all the figures and elements in the play. Or it could be an abstract composition in swirling colors to give the feeling of the final dance.

Some emotional-response compositions are made in collage form, with pieces of newspaper, string, sea-shells, spangles, and whatnot assembled into an interesting layout. The paper or drawing board should be large, about 24″ x 30″, to allow room for broad effects. Some emotional-response compositions are so attractive that they qualify as independent works of art, but their chief purpose is to help the director make a personal statement by objectifying an emotional reaction. If you prefer to work in three dimensions, try clay or plaster to present what your inner eye sees. Your first attempt will probably be frustrating because you lack the technique to express exactly what you dream, but more experience will enable you to design an effective composition. You will soon discover techniques of handling pattern, line, and color that will produce an emotional reaction from an observer who does not know the play you are analyzing.

Following the intellectual and intuitive steps of analysis comes the analysis of the play from a dramaturgical angle. The first step is to make a firm decision regarding the main plot and the sub-plots. The major and minor story lines must be made clear on the stage and projected cleanly and consistently. No interludes or elaborations, no matter how entertaining, should be allowed to interfere with the forward movement of the story. In *Lawyer Lincoln* the main plot is Lincoln's efforts to bring Keenie and Nate together, and there is only one sub-plot: the wager between Lincoln and the Judge. A three-act play may have several sub-plots to strengthen or highlight the main plot, but a one-act play usually has only one.

The sub-plots must be played in the same tone or mode as the main plot, but in a different key. In other words, a sub-plot should not sound or look as though it belonged to another play. For example, the Jessica-Lorenzo sub-plot in *The Merchant of*

Venice is light and exciting, but it has undercurrents and accents of potential bitterness in contrast to the actual bitterness of the main plot. The sub-plot complements and enhances the main plot, usually by contrast, but this contrast should be an integral part of the design for the whole play.

Many books on theatre and drama as literature will give help on dramaturgical analysis, but the new director can sharpen his tools by practicing on movies and TV shows. As he watches, he can ask himself these questions:

Is the theme of the play strong enough or interesting enough to hold my attention?

What devices does the author use to create mood or atmosphere?

Is the opening incident strong enough to seize my attention?

Are the important events of the play shown on stage, or are they merely described?

Is there a single character to whom the play belongs, or are there several interesting characters who dissipate an effect of unity?

Is there a definite beginning, middle, and end, or, if it is an avant-garde play, is the mood intense enough and are the situations varied enough to hold attention?

Does the dialogue move the play forward, or does it seem to go in circles?

Is the dialogue individualized so that it seems natural for each character?

Is the climax inevitable, or is it artificial and contrived?

Is the action justified by the nature of the people involved, or is it imposed arbitrarily?

Does the play give me insight into the human situation?

The best way to analyze a play is to discover whether or not it moves you and then go back over it to decide exactly what moments moved you and to determine whether it was something a character did or said or something that happened to a character. If all these moments are clear in your mind, the chances are good that you will make them clear on the stage for others to appreciate.

You can learn to read a play quickly at one sitting so that

you can experience its full impact. As you read, see the characters enter the stage and move about, and hear them as they speak their lines. In later readings you can find motivation for action and subtleties in characterization. The first reading should be continuous, which is the way the audience receives it. They can't go back over a page, and neither should you.

Try to analyze a play in terms of how effectively the author says what he wants to say, not in comparison with another play. Each play is a unique artistic entity and has its own rules built into it. Remember, however, that a play acts better than it reads because it was meant to be seen and heard.

If the director follows all these steps of analysis he should have a fairly complete understanding of the play. He should have an approach through which he will dramatize the meanings he has discovered. He should be able to interpret the play intellectually to his cast and theatrically to an audience. He should now be ready to prepare himself and the play for the first rehearsal, a process to be explained in the next chapter.

Chapter V

PREPARING FOR THE FIRST REHEARSAL

Now that the director has analyzed the play and knows what effects he wants and how to project those effects, he calls the crew heads together. At this meeting he distributes copies of the play and discusses his interpretation, but he leaves the field open for ideas from the crew heads. He also distributes and explains the production calendar, again asking for suggestions from his staff. It is a good idea to distribute copies of the ground plan or floor plan if it is ready.

The ground plan is a view of the setting from above, showing doorways, windows, steps, and location of furniture. It is drawn to scale, usually ¼″ on the plan equal to 1′ in real life. The director identifies the climax of the play and plans the ground plan around that moment, gradually adding furniture and space until all the needs of the play and the actors are met. He never adds furniture or doors that are not essential to the action.

He can have the designer or the stage crew draw up ground plans, but he should approve them before they are duplicated. The ground plan that comes with the published copy of *Lawyer Lincoln* is a good one and is reproduced here for our use. Following is the description of the room in which the play is set, taken from the play with permission of the publishers. The reader is reminded that Up Left Center means away from the audience (up), on the actor's left as he faces the audience and near the center of the back wall.

THE SETTING

Sis Beaseley's Boarding House in a Small Illinois Town.

The scene is a large, cheerful room, which has been made to serve as both living and dining room. The entrance from the out-

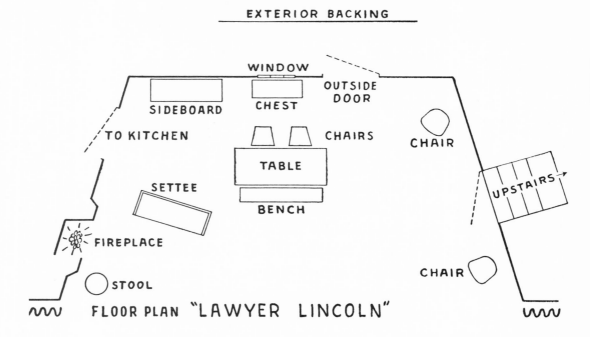

FLOOR PLAN "LAWYER LINCOLN"

side is Up Left Center in the back wall. Upstage in the Right wall is the door to the kitchen; and at Left, there is an opening to an unseen stairway leading up to the overhead rooms of the house. Under the small, high window to the right of the outside door, there is an old-fashioned chest. At Downstage Right is a wide fireplace, with a three-legged stool drawn up to it. At Right Center, a high-backed settee—facing front—forms a wing of a right angle to the fireplace. The long boarding table stands slightly upstage of Center, with two straight chairs in back of it and a narrow, backless bench in front of it. There are other chairs at Down Left and Up Left. (The sideboard shown in the sketch is optional.)

It is night. There is a blazing log fire in the fireplace and a lighted lamp on the table. The room has a softened, shadowy glow that is conducive to good cheer and good fellowship.

A comparison of the description and the drawing shows the location of each scenic unit required for the play. When I produce the play I shall make certain changes in the ground plan that I think will improve the visual aspects of the production. The back wall will be slanted (raked) to U.R. so that the fireplace wall is half again as long as the opposite wall. This device will make the room less boxlike in appearance and give it a feeling of greater warmth. I will remove the chair U.L., where it is too far upstage to be useful, and move the settee over to Left stage below the stair landing. I will place four steps and a landing on stage against the center of the Left wall so that actors walking up the steps can be easily seen as they leave. The Judge and Mr. Craig could retreat to the landing when the ladies' singing group enters. I will turn the table so that it runs up and down stage instead of sideways, to provide more acting space at Center.

Many play books include a ground plan of the setting, but it is more challenging and creative to develop an original set for a particular stage, cast, and auditorium. In any case, an entrance in the U.S. wall is desirable for *Lawyer Lincoln* so that Lincoln and other characters can make a visible and therefore impressive entrance. Other essentials are a table and chairs and a fireplace to show that this is a combination room.

The ground plan is important because it determines possibilities for picturization. Steps and levels give actors prominence and emphasis; furniture arranged in conversational groups allows actors to behave with apparent naturalness; and clear space is needed for entrances and exits, for such scenes as the square dance in *Lawyer Lincoln,* and for group and fight scenes.

If a play has many intimate scenes, furniture and fixtures such as a fireplace should be placed at the downstage corners of the stage so that the actors are near the audience.

In plays and musicals with many crowd scenes, it is necessary to know what is the center of interest at each moment and to train the actors to focus on it as it changes and never to look at the audience. For crowds of 24 or more it is wise to train certain leaders in location on the stage, motivation, and movement. The leaders then are responsible for training four to six chorus members in their action and business. The chief problem with chorus members is to keep them alert and listening and reacting properly through the long rehearsal period. The director should, if necessary, give each crowd-figure a distinct personality or characterization to think about so that he can listen and react as a real person, not an anonymous object.

Besides the ground plan, an important visual aid is a scale model of the setting. The model, usually made on a scale of ½″ to 1′, can be assembled from poster board. Or the director

*Keep singing soft
under this scene*
*Start demming lights
very slowly to
darken d L & d R
corners.*

LAWYER LINCOLN   19

*① she's angry but not
irritable*

KEENIE. No!

LINCOLN. Nate loves you. ①

KEENIE. Ain't enough. (*Stamps her foot again.*) I ain't takin' no man less'n he can make me a first-rate, bang-up proposal!

② *OK Lincoln encourages
Nate as man to man.*

LINCOLN. (*Puts his hand encouragingly on Nate's arm.*) Go ahead, Nate. (*Nate shakes his head stubbornly.*) You want to marry her? (*Nate shakes his head eagerly, indicating an affirmative. Lincoln ushers him downstage to front of fireplace.*) Ask her, then. ②

(*Nate shakes his head negatively. Keenie waits hopefully.*)

③ *plot line*

KEENIE. (*Pleadingly.*) ③ You got to ask me proper, or it'll get around that *I* done the proposin'. (*Nate sighs, shakes his head very sadly. She folds her arms and turns her back on him.*) All right! Don't!

LINCOLN. Just try it, Nate. Keenie'll meet you more than half-way, I'm sure.

④ *Nate starts low &
gradually increases
desperation*

OK - keep

(*She tosses her head but looks around slyly to see if he's going to use the suggestion. Nate, in stubborn but agonized ④ pantomime, indicates, "No." Lincoln sighs.*)

Well, I guess there's no hope for it. You won't propose, and she won't have you unless you do. I might as well give up. At least, the Judge will be pleased.

(*He turns to go. Frantically, Nate grabs him by the coattails and detains him. Lincoln stops and stares at Nate. The youth looks at him with such dumb pleading that Lincoln decides to try again.*)

⑥ *Lincoln & Nate X to
UC with Nate at R of
Lincoln — Keenie
still at L.C.*

⑤ *start of maj.
dimng.*

⑤ I reckon I've got to do the proposing, then. (*Nate seems delighted. Lincoln moves to left of Nate, takes his arm, and they ⑥ both cross to right of Keenie in front of bench.*) Miss Keenie . . . I ain't much on sweet talking. But I love you down deep, and I got a good farm that will take care of us in our old age.

KEENIE. (*Pertly.*) But I ain't old yet.

LINCOLN. Maybe Curly Allen's got a fancy way of speaking, but (*at the mention of Curly, Nate clenches his fist, frowns, and almost growls*) . . . he can't care for you like I do. (*Nate "fetches up" a deep sigh.*) No man could. Keenie, if you won't have me, I'm like to die. (*Nate looks very woebegone.*) Say you'll have me!

(*Nate hopefully holds out his hands toward her.*)

KEENIE. No. *Nate's* got to ask me, and I got to have the travelin' honeymoon.

LINCOLN. The honeymoon is assured. Nate will have money. He's going to serve on the—! (*Nate stops him, tugging des-*

can have a more permanent model of the stage house made of wood, which he can then use for all future designs. The model for the setting can be left unpainted so that the stage crew can discuss what colors to use. Stand-up paper figures scaled from 5′ to 6′ (2½″ to 3″ high for the model) can be made so that the director, by moving the figures around as the action progresses, can plan the movement pattern (blocking) of the play. The model, with simulated furniture and the figures in place, will be of immense help to crews and actors alike in visualizing the final effects desired by the director.

The next step in preparing for the first rehearsal is to make a director's script. This guide for rehearsal and performance is a large notebook with the pages of the playscript pasted on individual pages, leaving a wide margin for notes around the printed page. Another method is to cut a rectangular hole in the notebook pages the size of the printed area and paste the printed pages in place. In this method both sides of the printed page can be used and only one copy of the play is needed.

This notebook will be used at all rehearsals and performances as a prompt script, so it should be sturdy. It should also contain light cues and sound cues, ideas on characterization, motivation, and business that come to the director at odd moments, diagrams of movements and groupings, definitions of words or phrases, and a pattern of climaxes. All entries should be made in pencil so that changes during rehearsals can be incorporated. After the last performance, the director's script can serve as a record of the play, with photographs, a program, news stories, the lighting plot, and other documents added to it.

Mark the beginning of each crisis and the major climax with a wavy line in the margin. It is best to start with the main climax because it contains the whole point of the play and tends to be the moment the audience waits for. In *Lawyer Lincoln* the main climax or turning point is the embrace of Keenie and Nate. The buildup to it begins with Lincoln's line, "I reckon I've got to do the proposing, then." Minor climaxes as listed in Chapter IV should be marked off in a similar fashion. Too many plays are marred by an even, flat, monotonous pace with no ups and downs or builds and drops. It is important to mark the moments of tension and to remain aware of them during all rehearsals.

Next, mark the plot lines with a P.L. in the margin. Plot lines are speeches containing information the audience must have to follow the story. Examples of plot lines in the first half of *Lawyer Lincoln* are the following:

Sis: —and not even the first man of the jury picked yet.
Keenie: Maw said could we hold our Harmony class over to your house tonight?

A scene from an original play, We All Ganged Up on Everett Tuttle directed by Thomas J. Fenaughty at Teachers College, Columbia University. The actors illustrate interesting kinds of focus: direct and counter-focus on the boy at center, while two look at the store counter but remain "in the picture" because they are motionless. Justification or motivation for the boy's dominant position comes from the fact that he has a very important announcement to make. The observation platform and tele- scope at down right is outside the proscenium frame and helps the actors make close contact with the audience. This kind of contact is highly desirable in certain plays and should be employed when justified.

KEENIE: I ain't marryin' nobody less'n he can give me one of those new-style travelin' honeymoons.

NATE: (*Reluctantly*) It's . . . a gal.

JUDGE: —We've got to get a jury together.

LINCOLN: —You are never to lecture me again about wasting time.

JUDGE: —As a juror, you are not permitted to *talk* to anyone.

If the actors emphasize these lines properly, the audience will become involved and follow the last part of the play more easily.

Next the director adds diagrams of each movement and each grouping or picture. Since every arrangement of people and furniture on the stage is a composition, it might as well be a good composition with a meaning that projects to an audience, instead of a careless, random one. The grouping of people depends in part on their psychological relationship, and in part on the needs of the play. The director should know who is on whose side and why. If two characters are opposing one enemy, the two should normally stay together on one side of the stage, with the enemy on the other. The groupings or pictures should be so clear that a deaf person could get an idea of the play from just watching the action and reaction. Each moment in the play or musical should have its unique picture, and for every change of idea there should be a change of grouping. Certainly each unit in *Lawyer Lincoln* as we have divided it, and in all other productions, is a changed relationship and calls for a new grouping. But within each unit relationships change either subtly or obviously, and these changes should be reflected in small or large movement.

The blocking suggestions in the script of *Lawyer Lincoln* are good, and the directions should be followed carefully. However, since the motivations or reasons for movement are not included, they should be written into the margins to give to actors if necessary. For example, the book says that Lincoln moves to the chair D.L. (down-stage corner at actor's left) after he enters. No reason is given, but the actor must have a reason for absolutely everything he does on stage. The director could tell him that Lincoln wants to sit down and to put his tall hat next to the chair, in a safe place. Since the Judge and Mr. Craig oppose

A proposal scene from Rape of the Belt *directed by Paul Kozelka at Teachers College, Columbia University. Both actors are open to the audience so that they can be heard and seen easily, yet they relate strongly to each other. Masculine physical strength and feminine intellectual strength are here symbolized by the actions and attitudes of the characters.*

him, Lincoln chooses to sit on the opposite side of the room from them.

When the blocking is planned in advance, actors will not congregate in the center of the stage as they tend to do without a director. The center of interest changes constantly to various parts of the stage, but most important, the director can plan exactly who or what will be emphasized at any given moment. A television camera can focus on an actor's face as he speaks an important line, on the reaction of another actor as he responds to what is being said, or on an object that needs attention at the time. This kind of "zeroing in" cannot be done on the stage, but the director has at his disposal many other techniques of directing audience attention.

Among such techniques for securing emphasis are having everyone on stage turn face and body toward the person speaking (focus), having one person sit while the others stand or vice versa, framing a character in a doorway momentarily, and using downstage areas rather than upstage and center stage rather than the sides. Platforms (levels) and steps are excellent devices to raise an actor above the rest and give him emphasis. One character who is still while others are moving gives emphasis to the quiet one. In *Lawyer Lincoln* the actor playing Lincoln can be isolated and thus emphasized by coming D.L. while the other characters are on the opposite side of the stage. In his scene with Keenie and Nate, Lincoln stands between them and, because of his height, forms the apex of a triangle and is therefore an emphatic figure. The purpose of a triangular arrangement is to lead the audience's eye to a center of interest.

The first step in preparing the prompt script is to make cuts or changes in the script. Some changes will be made during rehearsals when you discover that an actor cannot make certain sounds or keeps stumbling over certain words. Swear words should be eliminated for most audiences. Words such as "damn" and "hell" and stronger ones are commonly heard in daily life, but on the stage and coming from neighbors or their children, swear words take on a new emphasis. This is especially true in amateur productions, in which the actors accent them out of all proportion to the rest of the line. Even Father's repeated expletive "Oh God!" in *Life with Father* can be offensive to some audiences and should be changed to "Oh Gad!" A good actor, if he is angry enough, can make a phrase like "jumping Jehosaphat" sound as juicy as any of Mark Twain's celebrated outbursts.

Long cuts in the script or extensive rewriting must be approved by the publisher of the play. Sometimes these changes will be approved if the reason is valid. The author is protected by copyright laws against alterations of his script, and the publisher's contract safeguards the author's rights.

Blocking for arena theatre is determined by the need of the audience to see faces as often as possible. Therefore, there is usually more movement in arena than in proscenium staging, but it still has to be motivated. The same principle applies: An actor is attracted to something or somebody and wants to come closer, or he is repelled and wants to move away. The ground plan for an arena production is always different from the one in the playbook. For *Lawyer Lincoln,* for example, the fireplace would have to be eliminated because it blocks the view; instead of the stairway, actors would use one of the aisles. The table could be in the center and extra benches or chairs placed around the edges of the playing area so that the townswomen could sit down and not block the view. During the proposal scene Keenie and Nate could sit on benches with the table between them while Lincoln paces around the entire acting area.

Some directors use a system of stage directions for arena theatre in which positions on the periphery are designated as points of the compass. Others use the figures of a clock to show stage positions. It is just as easy to tell an actor to go to the doorway or to the other side of the table, or to the hassock and have him diagram his path in his play script.

By moving the cutout figures of his actors on the model stage as he works out the movement pattern, the director can avoid the problem of one actor masking another from the audience. It is helpful, when the blocking is finished, to test it out by walking through the movements alone on the stage that will be used for the production. The director can then discover whether he has allowed enough time for a cross or other action to occur.

All diagrams and notes should be made in pencil so that they can be erased and replaced by ideas that come up during rehearsals. Sometimes the director has dreamed up some business that an actor cannot accomplish, and it must be changed. The actors often invent business or action that should become part of the prompt script. Notes made in ink look neater than pencil notes, but they cannot be altered.

By the time he has finished the prompt script, the director knows exactly what he needs in scenery, lighting, properties, and costumes; and he should then call a meeting of crew heads to discuss with them his ideas on how the play will look.

Some directors think that preparing a prompt book before rehearsals begin will cramp their creativity. As a matter of fact, working on the prompt book develops creativity. The task requires time, intense concentration, and a strong imagination. As he goes through the play the director hears and sees actors moving about the stage and indicates their changing positions in the margin. All the big movements should be charted in this way, with the small movements left for the actors to work out themselves.

Usually, crosses are straight diagonals for serious plays and melodramas and curved, graceful arcs for comedies, but this is an arbitrary rule with many exceptions. The best cross is the simplest, most direct path and the most comfortable move for the actor.

To prevent meaningless meandering, the director can add motivations for movement in the margin and then he is ready, for example, to tell the actor to cross to the chair down right *in order to* read the newspaper on the chair. The movement pattern in most plays is one of great activity and bustle at the beginning of the play and of less activity as the play moves toward its climaxes. *Lawyer Lincoln* needs much more movement in the opening scenes than it does in the long scene of Lincoln's proposal.

Most young actors are more comfortable moving and doing something rather than sitting still. The director should create meaningful, characterizing movement for his actors to help them convey attitudes and emotional states. Movement also helps in catching attention, and therefore it is very important to control it so that the attention falls on the right place at each moment.

Often a director can get an idea of the kind of movement to

A scene from Dulcy directed by Paul Kozelka at Teachers College, Columbia University. Footstools and hassocks are useful objects for actors. They encourage a comfortable, easy feeling in performers and spectators and permit variations in grouping for the director. A low bench or stool at the side of a stage can be used to keep an actor in an unobtrusive spot during a long scene in which he does not participate actively. The director should, nevertheless, keep an eye on him during rehearsals to see that he is listening constantly and reacting in small ways.

use as he watches his actors. He can incorporate a special walk or a unique movement and not resort to clichés.

Now we are ready to announce tryouts and to start rehearsing. Now the educational process begins and the director is ready to explain the finished product to his group by means of drawings, the model, and diagrams. The group must have an idea of the goal—the performance—as they begin the process that leads to that goal.

Chapter VI

TRYOUTS AND EARLY REHEARSALS

Attractive posters should be made advertising the name of the show and the time and place for tryouts. The posters can be made by the publicity crew. If possible, the tryouts should be held in the theatre where the show is to be given. The tryouts give an indication of the voice, stage presence, and acting ability of students. Thus it is desirable to use a theatre or large room to see if the candidate's voice carries and if there is a personal quality that is projected over a distance. Other qualities such as appearance and ability to move can also be discerned at a distance more easily than close up.

These are the general purposes of a tryout, but the method employed depends on the play and the number of people who show up.

If there are fewer than twenty, individual readings of five minutes each usually give satisfactory results. It is wise to use material other than the play that is to be presented. If the chosen play is used, the actors often set their hearts on a particular role and lose interest in the play as a whole. Monologues requiring varied emotional responses should be prepared, one set for males and one for females. These can be adapted from stretches of dialogue in standard plays, choosing a climactic or exciting moment. The actors should be given a few moments to study the lines before reading them.

Among the disadvantages of the individual method are: it takes more time than other methods, it may develop stage fright, and the student has no one with whom to react. However, the method is necessary when trying out for soloists for a musical.

A second method of tryouts is by pairs. When two persons work together stage fright is reduced, and they can at least begin to react to each other. Scripts can be drawn from several types of plays or from the play to be presented. The director may need to give a brief synopsis of the play, unless he uses opening scenes, which are self-explanatory. To test imagination, the director can ask each pair to improvise or pantomime a short scene, such as setting the table and serving a meal, purchasing an article, moving around a carnival lot, or watching a ball game. This type of exercise can, of course, be used with individuals as well.

A third way of handling tryouts is to invite four or five students up on the stage at one time. There is safety in numbers, and stage fright is greatly reduced. Tryout material for small groups may include improvisations or pantomimes and scenes with four or five characters chosen from standard plays.

If the aim is to discover talent and interest for several productions, a variety of materials should be used. Selections in prose and poetry and from light and serious works can be prepared in advance for the group. If a musical is being planned, candidates can sing a chorus of a popular song rather than a selection from the musical. It is important to choose appropriate material. The writer once used "Yankee Doodle" as tryout material, with disastrous results. Two girls from the South could hardly bring themselves to start the song and once started did not know how to finish it. From then on, only popular classics were used in tryouts.

Since most people become self-conscious when they walk up on a stage, the director is advised to watch candidates when they think they are not being watched. The director can divine important personality traits, mental attitudes, and degree of physical control as he watches a girl sitting with her friends waiting to be called and as she walks to and away from the stage. These are more or less intuitive but still reliable indicators. If there is time, the director can hold individual interviews to learn more about the actor's sensitivity, imagination, and responsiveness.

After the tryouts the director chooses a tentative cast and advertises it as such. In this way, he is free to make changes during the early rehearsals, should some of his guesses turn out wrong, without hurting anyone's feelings. He should also decide whether to use understudies or a double cast, as insurance against emergencies. Understudies in the educational theatre should have at least one chance to perform in public. Double casting can be wise when a wealth of talent is available and when the director can arrange his schedule to make the rehearsal period twice as long as usual. If a double cast is used, one should never be allowed to watch the other in rehearsal. The director will find that the two casts will develop two distinct interpretations of the same play. Audiences enjoy this, and often people come to performances of both casts. It is important, however, to keep the competitive spirit a constructive force.

The director is now ready for the first rehearsal, to which he brings his prompt book, a model of the setting, and possibly the drawing of his emotional response. With crew members and tentative cast seated around him, he explains his function as coordinator of the play—that he is in the driver's seat. He makes it clear that suggestions and ideas from the group are encouraged, but he should also make it clear that such suggestions should come before or after rehearsals, not during them. Rehearsal time is too valuable to be wasted on discussions or arguments. The director should begin to act like what he is: a benevolent dictator. Since he is responsible for the artistic success of the play, his vision, his interpretation, his judgment must prevail. At the same time, he is engaged in a creative process depending on the most subtle and powerful form of interpersonal relationships, so he cannot afford to be too autocratic, despotic, and joyless.

The director at this first rehearsal emphasizes the relationship between crews and cast, how interdependent they are, and how much the success of the production depends on both groups equally. He also stresses the necessity of being prompt for rehearsals and crew calls. He discusses the rehearsal schedule and makes sure that everyone understands it. It can be changed only if a majority of the group must attend an important event that conflicts with a rehearsal, and that the director did not know about. He explains how to notify him in emergencies. Then he makes a brief statement about the general problem of the play as he sees it.

Now it is time for him to be quiet and let the group begin to read the play. This should be a fast reading of the entire play to obtain an overall idea of its main features. The reading can

A scene from J. B. directed by Geraldine Staley, Illinois College, Jacksonville, Illinois. The physical arrangement of characters reveals psychological relationships.

be continuous around the circle with no one reading specific roles. If the cast stumbles and falters too much, the director can read the play aloud, but the cast can gain experience in reading aloud, no matter how unfinished the results. For a musical, the music is played and the libretto is read aloud. If the show is a mystery melodrama it is good business to swear the cast to secrecy about the outcome. If this is not possible, the last few pages of the script, which usually contain the solution of the problem, can be removed from each playbook and not rehearsed until far into the schedule.

At the second rehearsal, with the cast only, the director discusses with the group the meaning of the play and his analysis of it, at least that part of the analysis which concerns the actors. He discusses character relationships and the main conflicts. Then he distributes pencils and starts blocking Act I quickly, pausing only to give motivations for each movement, change of position, or regrouping. When the blocking for the first act is finished, the act should be run through again to help set it in the actors' minds. It is wise to get these mechanics of movement established as early as possible, to enable the actors to concentrate on building character and developing reaction patterns. Again, at this second rehearsal, the director should work hard on developing the right atmosphere for creative exploration by his actors. He should be ready to answer any question at any rehearsal by any actor unless he thinks the problem will take care of itself in a subsequent rehearsal. The French word for rehearsal is *répétition*, and rehearsal time should be spent repeating the lines and action of the play, not wasted in fruitless discussions.

At the second rehearsal of a musical, the principals and chorus should work in separate rooms on the blocking and music.

The third rehearsal should take place on the stage or in a room large enough to provide the playing space shown on the floor plan. The assistant director or a member of the stage crew can mark off the location of doors and walls with chalk or masking tape so that the actors can get an idea of space limitations as soon as possible. One of the purposes of rehearsals is to make the actors comfortable and at home on the stage. Hence, they should work as early in the schedule and as often as possible on the stage itself or in an equivalent space. If they rehearse in a small room until the dress rehearsal, they will look awkward and unprepared on the stage.

In the third rehearsal, the first act should be repeated quickly and without interruptions, purely for review. The director should watch to see how the stage areas are used and whether the actors are comfortable in their movements. Then Act II should be blocked and, if there is time, repeated.

For *Lawyer Lincoln* the cast would have blocked the play and repeated it several times during the first two rehearsals, and the third rehearsal might be spent on the long scene between Lincoln, Keenie, and Nate. Each line, action, and reaction should be thoroughly discussed and analyzed so that the actors know exactly what the characters are thinking at every moment.

In the fourth rehearsal Act III should be blocked and repeated immediately. There should be time to begin work on the buildup and the climax, which usually come in this act. The cast should know where the turning point is and by what means it will be projected to the audience. It is time, also, to begin discussions of characterization. The actors now have an idea of the changes that occur in each character during the play, and they might begin using props such as a cane, a shawl, an unlighted pipe, or a hat to help them begin to understand how another personality thinks, feels, and acts.

For *Lawyer Lincoln* many of the lines should be memorized by this time, and evidences of a beginning characterization should appear. If the cast still seems like a group of strangers, the director should try an improvisation. He might have the cast imagine they are townspeople who come to the General Store to purchase or barter specific items, or who gather on the Village Green for a celebration or contest; or they might be modern apartment dwellers who all meet on the sidewalk for a fire drill or air-raid drill.

The fifth rehearsal should be given over to a complete run-through of the play or musical. It is important for many reasons for the cast to get an idea of the play as a whole. By listening to the full play they get ideas about their characters' development from beginning to end. They also learn to save energy for the last act, usually the most strenuous and certainly the most critical. This rehearsal is important for the director, too, because he can decide, after seeing the whole play, whether any part needs to be cut out or adapted in some way. Perhaps there is needless repetition, unnecessary exposition, or a series of difficult words that the actors stumble over.

The fifth rehearsal is important for another reason. After this session the director should make a final decision about the cast and let the actors know definitely whether they are to keep their roles or be replaced. When replacing an actor it is best to assure him or her that the change has nothing to do with acting ability, but that he does not quite have the qualities necessary for this role with this particular group of actors. The director should soften such a blow to the ego if he possibly can.

By the fifth rehearsal of a one-act play such as *Lawyer Lincoln* all actors should know their lines. Even though some actors memorize quickly and others are very slow, a firm deadline should be stated on the rehearsal schedule by which all lines should be learned. The deadline for a long play should be the tenth rehearsal.

Memorizing often occurs automatically during rehearsals, but many times an actor must sit down by himself and study his lines. He must be exact and not memorize halfway. The end of each speech especially—the cues—must always be spoken exactly, so that other actors know when to come in. The director should insist on perfect memorization; it is unfair to playwright and audience to speak lines that are almost right. Some actors like to memorize with a tape recorder, recording their cues and leaving empty spaces on the tape in which they recite their own lines. Other actors hold a card over the printed page and expose only their cues. In any case, the student should understand the main idea of a scene and then discover how the author develops the idea through a series of progressing speeches. He should always memorize aloud in order to get used to the sound of his own voice.

Rehearsals six, seven, eight, nine, and ten should be divided equally among the three acts. They should emphasize getting well acquainted with the play, starting memorization, developing characterization, learning to react, and deciding on definite positions for every moment of the play. There should be at least

A rehearsal of **The Potting Shed** directed by *W. Scott McConnell at Teachers College, Columbia University. The assistant director takes notes while some actors perform and others wait for their entrance cues. Actors can learn a lot about their characters and about the play as they listen to other characters. Rehearsals give actors a chance to try out business and other characterizing devices they have thought up. Repetitions can be fascinating to the director as he sees his actors incorporate suggestions he has made. Rehearsals require intense concentration by the director and actors, and all distracting elements should be eliminated.*

one complete run-through in this series. There will probably be some rehearsals for the principals only or for certain scenes that are particularly difficult.

During this series of rehearsals, the director should interrupt whenever it is apparent that an actor does not understand what he is saying. Find out what the actor thinks the line means, and if he is right, help him bring out the meaning with a pause, a reaction, a piece of business, a movement, a sudden change of volume, or some other technique. If he is wrong, help him grasp the meaning by an analysis of the words, by paraphrasing the lines, by showing the relation of this speech to others in the play, by revealing the hidden meaning in the lines, or by having the actor's partner read the lines once or twice. If necessary, give the line reading yourself, but not until all other attempts have failed. Since the actors are beginning to memorize, it is important that they learn the correct line readings; if they memorize the wrong ones, they will have a hard time unlearning them.

The director can begin to study transitions between the units of the play during this series of rehearsals. Are they clear and cleancut and beginning to acquire smoothness? Do the actors show a change of thought or mood? Is this change manifested in some physical way? It will be helpful during this period for the director to refer to the lists of actions prepared for each actor during analysis of the prompt script. Rather than telling the actor directly what he is supposed to be thinking and doing, it is more satisfactory to draw it out of him inductively by questions.

The most important objective for rehearsals six through ten is clarity of character relationships. Each actor should understand exactly how his character feels about every other character in the play at every moment. This attitude should be clearly projected so that the audience will understand it. For example, Sis Beaseley's manner is different toward every character in *Lawyer Lincoln,* but more important is the fact that in her scene with Nate she changes several times in her manner or attitude toward him. This ability to perceive and project the dynamics of interpersonal relationships is the essence of acting. And it is part of the director's responsibility to keep his actors aware of the dynamic tensions written into every good play. The

A scene from Twelfth Night directed by Carol Brinser at the Senior High School, Westfield, N.J. The actors rehearsed in their costumes enough times to act in them with ease and authority. Character relationships are manifested through posture and facial expression.

director can help the actors by getting them to recall certain incidents or relationships that parallel, to some degree at least, those in the play. The girl who plays Sis Beaseley, for example, may not be a mother herself but she has had motherly feelings toward her dolls. If asked what she would do if she *were* Sis Beaseley, she would say she would have a motherly, hospitable feeling for everyone who came to her boarding house. Then if the image of her attitude toward her own dolls or pets is brought out she can use this image in building her characterization.

Women directors are sometimes more sensitive to interpersonal relationships than men; therefore, men directors often consult women whose opinions they respect when analyzing plays with complex male-female relationships. This type of consultation should help a director explain motivations and attitudes to his cast. With the possible exception of this one area, it does not matter whether the director is a man or a woman, provided he or she has all the other qualities necessary for the job.

The tenth rehearsal of a short play such as *Lawyer Lincoln* should be a dress rehearsal, with all props, scenery, costumes, and lights ready for use. The play can be gone through twice at this rehearsal so that the cast can benefit from the experience.

With beginning actors it is best to schedule rehearsals as frequently as possible. If they meet every day they will remember what they learn at each rehearsal. If they meet only once or twice a week, they lose a lot of time at the beginning of each session just getting themselves to the proper pitch, and they may forget what they learned a week earlier.

The director's attitude can be a strong factor in setting the tone of a rehearsal. He should be an attentive audience, concentrating on what is going on and quietly making notes. He should not interrupt unless absolutely necessary. Actors cannot get their teeth into a scene or feel the surge of it if they have to stop every few minutes. The director may be tempted at an early rehearsal to stop a scene and get a climax going toward a high pitch, but he should realize that the actors will develop the climax when characters are fully understood and lines are learned.

The director should be quick to praise accomplishment and growth and slow to lose his temper or show impatience if an actor does not learn fast enough. The actors must believe that the director has faith in them and is always on their side. Of course, an actor who is late at rehearsals, is too lazy to learn lines, or causes distractions should be reprimanded immediately. If he does not change his habits after one warning, he should be replaced. If an actor has an emergency he should notify the director, who can then make adjustments in the rehearsal plan.

Some community theatre groups look on rehearsals as social occasions. It is then up to the director to demonstrate through his own example and through tactful explanation that rehearsals are serious business.

It is usually necessary to call a short break for relaxation after every hour of rehearsals. The intense concentration required can be very exhausting. Therefore, rehearsals should not run longer than two or two and a half hours.

After each rehearsal the director and actors should have a feeling that something positive has been achieved and that the play has moved closer to a finished product. After a monotonous rehearsal or line drill, the director should point out that the actors have moved forward even though they have spent the time on mere repetition, explaining that mastery of lines leads to greater freedom and intelligence in delivering them. This should restore the actor's sense of progress.

Chapter VII

KEY REHEARSALS

The eleventh rehearsal should be a complete run-through of the play with no books permitted. All lines should be memorized, and it should be a relatively smooth rehearsal. This run-through will give the entire cast the experience of hearing and seeing the whole play. Individual members may get ideas for their characterization as they hear themselves talked about in scenes in which they do not take part. Also, an uninterrupted run-through helps the actors to realize how little time there is between their appearances on the stage. The assistant director can prompt as the actors require it.

The director has many things to watch for in this run-through. He is interested in any rough spots. These usually are caused by faulty transition from one scene to another, by failure of the actors to sustain their characters, and especially by their failure to listen to each other. By this time all motivations and character relations should be clear to the actors and to the viewer. If they are not, the director makes note of the weak spots and talks to the cast, either after each act or at the end of the play. This rehearsal should give him the basis for determining the nature and number of the remaining rehearsals.

Rehearsals twelve to twenty are the critical ones and for most plays require the attendance of the entire cast so that run-throughs can be held regularly. By this time it is too late for experimenting with interpretation and characterization. Small experiments in timing and tone color are still permitted, of course, to keep spontaneity, but not large ones. These rehearsals should be spent polishing business and drilling on action until both are smooth and clear.

If necessary, the director can give exact line readings and demonstrate how a bit of business or action should be done. An actor may need this kind of assistance, and he should receive it

A scene from Saint Joan *with Genevieve Bujold and Roddy McDowall in the NBC-TV Hallmark Hall of Fame production. Listening with complete concentration is the hardest and most important job of the actor.*

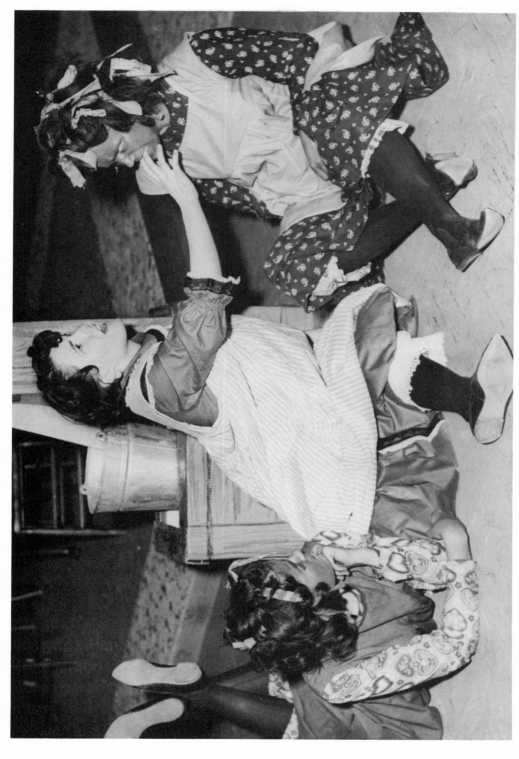

A scene from The Miracle Worker *directed in arena style by Sister Mary Angelita Kramer, BVM, at Our Lady of Peace High School, Saint Paul, Minnesota. Action and reaction are as intense in arena theatre as they are for proscenium theatre but not so large.*

if he has tried his own way unsuccessfully. During this period, one run-through can be recorded or put on video tape so that the cast can get an accurate—if painful—idea of how they are getting across. This device will underscore what the director has been saying for several weeks, but the learning comes from a new source. Another form of reinforcement is a recording of the play by a professional company. Such a recording can be played in this series of rehearsals without destroying the students' creativity; it can give them an objective view of the play and demonstrate acting techniques at the same time.

Picking up of cues is another important technique that must be learned at this time. Inexperienced actors often wait after each cue to take a breath and then come in with their line. These repeated pauses create a dull, slow performance. Actors need to be drilled on the technique of taking a breath on a certain word or phrase in the speech before their cue, and beginning their line with a strong attack at the instant the preceding speech is finished. Actually, the audience gets the impression that the lines overlap, and they remain alert and attentive. However, if the director expects a laugh at the end of a certain line, he will have the cue picked up not with a speech but with a reaction, a movement, or business.

Some actors develop a habit of coming in too soon and overlapping their line with the cue; this is frustrating to the other actor and to the audience as well. At times, of course, overlapping is desirable because it adds excitement to a scene. It should be used when the words themselves are not important or are repetitious. It is an effective technique for argument or fight scenes.

Some actors pick up their cues on time but ease into each speech so softly that they cannot be heard. These actors should be taught to attack each opening phrase briskly. This is especially important when the speech begins with "but" or "if." The audience must hear these words in order to understand the implications of the whole speech.

Another factor to watch for in this rehearsal series is the uniqueness of each actor's speech pattern. After hearing each other for several weeks of rehearsal, actors begin to pick up

A chorus scene from Oklahoma! directed by Mrs. Janie Yates at A. L. Brown High School, Kannapolis, North Carolina. This musical is very popular with performers and audiences because of its strong story line and beautiful music.

each other's volume level and rate of speaking. This is dangerous because it leads to an unspontaneous effect, whereas conversation is always spontaneous. The actors can correct this difficulty if they listen to their voices recorded on tape or if the director calls their attention to it. Another irritating problem occurs when one actor speaks softly and his partner speaks in a loud voice. After a while the audience becomes tired of adjusting to the contrasting sound levels and tunes out.

The director may discover during the key rehearsal period that two actors playing an intimate scene cannot project this intimacy in a large auditorium, even though they captured it when rehearsing in a small room. The solution to this problem is to rehearse the scene over and over but separate the actors gradually until they are thirty feet apart. The distance will force them to articulate more clearly and to place their voices near the front of the mouth, so that when near each other they can be loving and tender and still be heard.

The director should check on variations of tempo throughout the play. If a scene is not playing right, the actors may be speaking too fast or too slow for the best interpretation of the scene. The director should work until he finds the right tempo for each scene and then drill the cast so that they achieve that tempo for every rehearsal. Usually fast and slow scenes alternate, but it all depends on the play. The proposal scene in *Lawyer Lincoln*, for instance, starts slowly but ends with a rush. If necessary, the director can break the pattern of full run-throughs by drilling on one act for an entire rehearsal if it seems necessary. His aim during this period is to achieve smoothness in the performance and authority in his performers. This can be achieved only through constant repetition, so that complete familiarity results. If necessary he can restrict one rehearsal to work on lines exclusively. The cast members sit in a circle, with the lights either on or off, and shoot the lines back and forth as quickly as they can. In plays such as *Inherit the Wind*, in which the crowd scenes are so important, the director might devote one rehearsal in this series only to members of the crowd.

It is advisable to work with costumes as much as possible in this period, or at least with costume substitutes. The cast must look as though they were brought up in the costumes they are wearing. Plays such as *The Importance of Being Earnest, The Rivals,* and *Amahl and the Night Visitors* should be rehearsed often in costume so that the costumes become a part of the actors.

Needless to say, the stage should be used as often as possible for this series of rehearsals, and the director should move around to different parts of the theatre or arena to check the visibility and projection of his actors. He reports on his findings at the end of each act or at the end of the rehearal. In a play such as *Blue Denim* he might want to work on the love scenes in private. Adolescents playing love scenes feel more comfortable in someone's living room instead of working in front of a large group of their peers. Embraces and kisses should be rehearsed so often that the young people lose every trace of self-consciousness in their actions.

The director's attitude is important during this last group of rehearsals. He should maintain a critical attitude as though seeing the play for the first time. He himself knows that certain members of the cast have made tremendous gains during the rehearsal period, but the audience does not care about this therapeutic value. They care about seeing fully developed characters acting out a believable story. In other words, the director must bring his cast up to performance level if he ever hopes to get away from the indulgent, apologetic attitude of many audiences toward amateur productions. If monotony creeps into the rehearsal period, the director should be ready with encouragement of some kind to bring his actors back to fresh responses. Sometimes the play seems dead because it has been over-rehearsed; that is, the actors have stopped listening, stopped acting, and are simply reciting lines. Perhaps a good improvisation will solve the problem. Or the director can reverse the order of playing and start with Act III for one rehearsal.

This period is difficult for the director as well as for the actors. Because he has seen the play so often, it is hard for him to come to it with a fresh view, but he must remain attentive during rehearsals. His criticisms are extremely important to the future of the play, and he should take great care in his choice of words so that the cast understands him completely. If time is short and there is not room for enough run-throughs, the di-

A scene from Take Her, She's Mine directed by Julien R. Hughes at Leuzinger High School, Lawndale, California. By using the triangle principle, the two groups of actors give focus and emphasis to the actors who are telephoning. The actors are comfortable but alert, as the result of long rehearsals.

rector may schedule simultaneous rehearsals under his assistants. These can contribute smoothness to the performance by giving more time for repetition. If the director sees a need for special coaching on voice, or body work, or complicated business, he should arrange separate rehearsals for these problems. Above all, he should understand the job of the actors, empathize with them as they build up to the big event, and do his utmost to keep them calm. The best way to keep a group of actors calm is to give them the feeling of self-confidence that comes only from thorough familiarity with the play.

Needless to say, no visitors should be allowed at rehearsals. Young actors begin to show off when they have an audience too soon. They strain for results, they want approval but have not yet earned it.

Actors should not be called if they are not needed at a particular rehearsal. If the schedule shows that Act II is to be rehearsed on Monday and Tuesday but the director discovers that only the principal characters need more work on Act II, he can announce on Monday that only the principals are needed the next day. As an alternative, he can work with the principals on Tuesday while his assistant rehearses the minor players in another room.

After the lines have been memorized, the director should gradually introduce properties such as cups and saucers, canes, handkerchiefs, and pipes so that the actors can incorporate business or action with speech. An actor can be surprisingly clumsy when he handles properties for the first time. Actors should be encouraged to work on handling properties at home instead of taking time at rehearsals. Nate in *Lawyer Lincoln* can practice his eating scene at home where he will have real meat to chew on instead of the sliced apples, bread, and sliced beets he will probably have for performance. He can practice until the timing of speaking and eating is under control and he is in no danger of having his mouth full when he hears a cue.

All the actors should be encouraged to work on their characterizations between rehearsals. They can observe people on the street and notice distinctive ways of walking and talking. The girls playing Sis Beaseley and the townswomen in *Lawyer Lincoln* should observe older women as they walk, shop, cook

Molière's The Doctor in Spite of Himself directed by Jean Anderson at Burlingame (California) High School. If properties are at hand for rehearsals, business can be integrated smoothly with speech.

A scene from The House of Bernarda Alba *directed by Eugene Bence at Memphis (Tennessee) State University. Strong emotional scenes require strong actions and reactions. This is the kind of play for which actors should be encouraged to write autobiographical sketches of their characters.*

a meal, and put on hats and coats. The boy playing Lincoln must observe many men around forty years of age to see how differently their bodies move compared to the actions of a teenager. Little details like holding the head at a certain angle (in order to hear better), or a particular way of holding the hands, or mannerisms in facial muscles or in body movement, or a unique way of gesturing for emphasis are observable and can be imitated. Of course, the actor should justify each detail he uses. He should incorporate such details during key rehearsals to enrich his characterization, not simply to experiment.

The actors should be encouraged and sometimes required to

write a complete autobiography of their character, including his past life and all the events not shown on the stage. This sketch can help the actor to enrich the characterization and convey subtly to the audience that the character has an off-stage life as well as on-stage one.

The actors can do other things between rehearsals to improve their characterizations. They can listen to their voices on portable tape recorders, which are now available for around ten dollars. They can read other plays by the same author to explore his philosophy. They should read the whole play often in order to keep their role in its proper relation to the rest of the characters. When actors concentrate on a single role, they may lose sight of the way it fits into the full tapestry.

By the end of this period of key rehearsals the cast should be able to go through the play with mounting tension and energy so that the climactic third act is indeed as effective as the author intended.

To test his judgment and to help the actors, the director might invite a very small group of people—perhaps ten—to watch the final rehearsal in this series, before the dress rehearsals begin. By sitting with the guests, watching their responses, questioning them, and discussing the performance with them, he can learn which scenes are effective and which are not. The guests should be sophisticated enough to visualize the missing costumes, scenery, and lighting effects. Nevertheless, this open rehearsal can be amazingly powerful precisely because there are no distracting or supportive elements.

The cast, too, will be stimulated by a small audience and will probably give an excellent performance. If the rehearsal goes badly, the cast is probably having opening-night jitters—which means they will escape them on opening night.

This rehearsal should be very useful to the director by giving him an idea of the rhythm of the play. A palpable rhythm is inherent in every good play and is achieved by accents or moments of emphasis that occur in some kind of regular pattern. A serious play has a pattern of relatively heavy beats, and a comedy has a number of light but pronounced accents. Sometimes a certain word or phrase, connected to the theme of the play, is repeated regularly. Sometimes the accent is less obvious and is an idea repeated in paraphrase. In semiritualistic plays the rhythm can develop from repeated groupings or movement. By studying paintings, either abstract or realistic, and by listening to symphonies, both modern and classical, the director can develop a sensitivity to rhythm that will help him discover it in a play. The difference between tempo and rhythm is that fast and slow tempos are easy to spot, rehearse, and project, whereas rhythm is more subtle. It can consist of heavy or light beats, staccato or broad accents, alternating long and short beats, and it can be aided by costume touches, elements in the scenic design, and accents in lighting.

It should be added that a play's rhythm often develops by itself if the tempo of each unit or scene is correct and if the transitions from one unit to the next are smooth and distinctive. If Shakespeare's plays are presented as they were written, with one scene flowing rapidly into the next, a good rhythm is achieved automatically.

If the units in *Lawyer Lincoln* are played with the variety each should have to distinguish it properly from its neighbors, the performance will have an organic rhythm that builds with growing intensity to the whirling square dance at the end. The rhythm in this play and any other play would be distorted if a series of stage waits occurred. A stage wait is an accidental pause in the action caused by some kind of error. An actor fails to enter on time, or forgets his lines, or loses a prop, or drops out of character, and for a seemingly interminable moment nothing happens. A dramatic pause, on the other hand, is a long or short moment of such high intensity that words are unnecessary. The character is making a tremendous decision, or he is finally comprehending something of vast importance, or his relationship to another character is changing completely and he needs time for the realization to sink in.

Actors and directors and playwrights know the value of dramatic pauses and sometimes overuse them. Too many pauses are unjustified; they slow up the play and begin to look like stage waits.

It is during the period of key rehearsals that the director watches the pattern of dramatic pauses and decides whether there are enough or too many, and whether they are as significant as he wants them to be. Actors tend to make them too short because they are afraid of losing the audience. The director can count out loud to demonstrate to the actors how many seconds the pause should last. He also should check carefully on what the actor is thinking during the pause. Without powerful thinking by the actor, the pause becomes a stage wait.

The relation of dramatic pauses to the rhythm of a play becomes apparent to the director as he watches the key rehearsals objectively. He might devote his attention to this and other techniques of acquiring rhythm during one rehearsal in the series and put aside temporarily his other responsibilities as outlined in this chapter.

If rehearsals have progressed as they should, the group is now ready for dress rehearsals and performance.

Chapter VIII

DRESS REHEARSALS AND PERFORMANCE

It is assumed that costume fittings have been going on all during the key-rehearsal period, coordinated with the rehearsal schedule by the assistant director. If possible, publicity photos should be made showing crews at work with actors rehearsing in the foreground. The pictures should be clear and with good contrasts so that they will reproduce well in newspapers. For morale purposes it is wise to include secondary actors with the leads. A good photographer can take interesting action shots during a rehearsal showing the director and actors at work. Action shots are natural and unposed and have high publicity value.

The first dress rehearsal should be a technical rehearsal during which the scenery, lights, sound effects, and props are tried out. In preparing for it, the director checks with the crew heads to be sure that all is in readiness. If the show is a complicated one such as a musical, only the crews are present at the technical rehearsal; they go through the whole show slowly and deliberately, seeing how everything works and making notes on cue sheets for lighting and scenic and sound effects. If the show is relatively simple scenically, the actors may be present and have another chance to go through the whole play, but slowly and with interruptions, because this rehearsal is intended especially for the technical people. The director watches carefully to see that doors open and close properly, that sound effects come at the proper time, that the lighting makes figures visible, that scene changes are prompt, and that the curtains open and close at the proper speed.

Costumes are added for the second dress rehearsal, and the director checks the effect of lights on them. The actors become accustomed to moving and sitting in their costumes and find ways to make them part of the characterization. A dress parade should be held during this rehearsal when each actor stands at

119

A publicity shot from the stage reading of Getting Married, directed by Paul Kozelka at Teachers College, Columbia University. The entire cast is grouped closely, with just enough action to create interest. Newspaper readers like to identify their friends, so the more people who can be crowded legitimately into a photograph the more people will look at it.

In this production, actors carried books and spoke their memorized lines from a reader's desk for the first half of the play. In the second half they moved around in front of the desks without books and acted out the plot.

A publicity shot for The Skin of Our Teeth *directed by Carol Brinser at the Senior High School, Westfield, N.J. An interesting family portrait attracts attention and arouses curiosity about the play.*

Screen scene from School for Scandal *directed by Paul Kozelka at Teachers College, Columbia University. For a period piece, actors should begin to wear wigs and items of costume as soon as possible. They will look stiff and awkward unless they have time to grow into a costume. When renting costumes, it is worth the extra cost to have them for an extra week so that the actors can adjust to them and the publicity crew can take pictures.*

center stage and under stage lights while the costume crew head and the director scrutinize his costume.

For the third dress rehearsal makeup can be added and curtain calls rehearsed. This rehearsal should be fairly smooth compared to the first two dress rehearsals with all their distractions, and the actors should work hard to recapture the intensity they had achieved in the key-rehearsal period. Crew members should be invited to see as much of this rehearsal as they can from out front. For a one-act play such as *Lawyer Lincoln*, it is

Jean Simmons and Keith Mitchell in two stages in their lives in Soldier in Love *for the NBC-TV Hallmark Hall of Fame production. Make-up is especially important in arena theatre to transform young people to older ones. Other aids to characterization are posture, voice, and mental attitude.*

possible to achieve the aims of the three rehearsals just described in one session, combining scenery, lights, props, costumes, and makeup for the first time.

Curtain calls must be planned and rehearsed so that the audience leaves with a good final impression. For a large cast, groups can come out from the wings quickly, take a bow, and retire upstage, with the principal figures forming the last group. It is not necessary to have curtain calls for individuals, since their success is primarily the result of group effort. For the second and last curtain call, members of the various crews can come out for a bow if they have been rehearsed. For *Lawyer Lincoln* it is suggested that the whole cast line up off-stage with Lincoln as the central figure, and that they all walk in swiftly, stop when Lincoln is at center stage, turn, hold hands, and bow twice. The curtains close and, if the applause warrants it, open again for bows. In no case should curtain calls be used to present gifts or flowers over the footlights to certain members of the cast. The appreciation of the audience and the experience of working in the play are sufficient rewards.

Now comes the fourth dress rehearsal, for which all performance conditions are reproduced except that there is no audience. The cast must be dressed and made up at least ten minutes before the scheduled time. The stage manager announces "half hour," "ten minutes," and "places for act one," and the actors quietly obey. At this point the stage manager has absolute authority backstage. The director's job is finished, and he should stay in the auditorium, leaving all details to the production crew under the stage manager. It is important to point out again that students react very well to responsibility if they know what is required of them and that they have true, not partial, responsibility.

For the fifth and final dress rehearsal a small preview audience, either of students or adults, should be invited. They can sit together in the center of the auditorium, with the director nearby to watch for reactions. This small group will motivate the actors to perform at their peak and will provide valuable responses to the director.

The five dress rehearsals might be scheduled as follows: technical-dress on Sunday afternoon, second dress rehearsal on Mon-

Scene from The Potting Shed directed by W. Scott McConnell at Teachers College, Columbia University. The setting is small but provides room for comfortable movement and for six characters to be seated. The upstage levels permit interesting triangular groupings, and the actors take emphasis in turn by the way they speak and listen. It is sometimes desirable to associate a stage location or piece of furniture with a certain character in the play to help the audience understand character relations. Thus, the window seat is used only by the young daughter, and when she is off stage the seat recalls her presence.

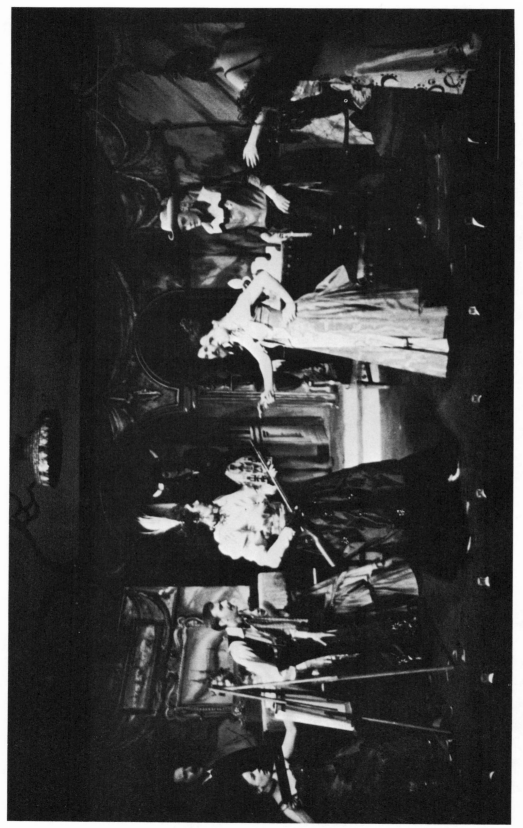

A turbulent moment from an original play, The Age of Opulence or Sham! directed by Barbara H. Battle at Teachers College, Columbia University. The two chief figures in a fight scene are at center stage. The other characters focus on the action while they freeze (remain motionless) in position. Any movement on their part would detract from the tension of the scene.

This play, like all spoofs, must be acted sincerely by the actors. They have to take themselves and their actions seriously but add just enough exaggeration and zest to clue the audience into the entertainment values of the play.

day evening, third on Tuesday, fourth on Wednesday, preview on Thursday, and opening night on Friday. This schedule provides a continuous buildup to opening night. The cumulative effect should not be broken to let the cast rest for a day. Such a delay can be fatal to energy level, enthusiasm, tempo, and general tension. Inclusion of the preview helps to avoid opening-night nerves and to provide a smooth, professional performance.

The director needs to communicate with cast and crews during this set of rehearsals, and he can do it in several ways. One effective way is to call everyone together on stage after the curtain call and go through his notes. Another way is to prepare a set of notes to be posted on a bulletin board and read just before the next rehearsal. In either case everyone knows what changes have been ordered, and no one will be surprised when they are incorporated into the performance. Another way to communicate, especially if the group is a large one, is to call together the crew heads and the assistant director, give them the messages, and let them in turn notify the crew members and actors.

What might these messages be? Only rarely would they call for a special rehearsal to make major changes in movement or business. This should have been done the preceding week, if necessary. Usually the messages run something like this, with notes following the character's name, not the actor's.

Lincoln: Very good performance tonight, but you didn't enjoy being with people—Lincoln was moody, but in this play he is spirited and stimulating.

Sis: Cover bobby pins in hair piece or wear net—safety-pin shows in hem—use apron to wipe off table.

Nate: Better than last night, but I lost some speeches because you slurred the words together—stay shy, but speak more distinctly.

Keenie: Very good tonight, but spoke too fast in your first scene—remember, you are out of breath from running.

Judge: Very impressive appearance and manner, but beard too thick and therefore unrealistic—don't use so much crepe hair.

Everyone: Slow, ragged entrance for curtain calls. Be

lined up backstage in time and follow stage manager's directions, especially the one on keeping quiet backstage. Performance on the whole was pretty good, but the feeling of 1849 was not there as it was last night. Use some will power and imagination before you come on stage. Think hard about the things your character would have done that day, the thoughts you might have had, the people you might have talked with, the conversations you might have had. Think about what you had for supper (except Nate) and smell the corn muffins, baked ham, hominy grits, fresh milk, and spiced apples. Bring the spirit of 1849 in with you, don't wait for it to arrive after you have entered.

A certain person came on stage chewing gum. If you are that nervous, it means you are thinking about yourself and not about the play.

Stage Manager: Let me know if anyone is late tonight. Thanks for remembering to fix the squeaking door hinge. Curtain started to close one beat too soon. We all appreciate the way you are doing your job.

Presumably, performances are given on Friday and Saturday evenings for two successive weekends. A run-through for lines only will probably be necessary on Thursday of the second week. At this time the director can introduce small changes (not major ones) based on audience reactions, such as building laughs with business instead of freezing (holding a position) during every laugh, varying tempos, and making slight changes in characterizations, focus, and emphasis.

To keep morale high, the director should visit the cast before each performance, checking on voices and general physical condition of each person connected with the show. During the performance the director remains in the audience to watch the play and to observe audience response. This experience will help him tremendously as a director, enabling him to learn what is successful and what is not in terms of his specific public. He will also be encouraged and intrigued by the artistic growth of his actors as they perform before different audiences.

Performing before an audience of teen-agers or young children has both rewards and hazards. Accustomed to constant

Scene from Fresh Fields, showing an overcrowded stage. The play was directed by Paul Kozelka at Teachers College, Columbia University. The furniture arrived only in time for dress rehearsal, and by then it was too late to make substitutions. The actors had to make adjustments in movement patterns, sometimes smoothly, sometimes awkwardly. The sofa was too long and destroyed the effectiveness of the center entrance. All the furniture was rented, so nothing could be done about clashing colors. If at all possible, a group that produces plays regularly should collect basic furniture that can be repainted or re-covered for each production. The actors, then, will be able to use the final furniture at early rehearsals. A note in the program requesting articles of furniture and costume accessories will produce astonishing results. The problem, of course, is to store and classify all the theatre's possessions.

A scene from **Peter Pan** *directed by Edward Ragozzino at South Eugene High School, Eugene, Oregon. Children who can act contribute enormously to the believability of a play because of their naturalness and spontaneity. Children, not adults, should always be used in child roles.*

action and a high level of sound on television, young audiences get restless if they cannot hear and if there is not constant action on the stage. The cast should be prepared for such an audience. Warn them to come on firm and strong, to speak with a little extra volume, and to exert all the authority of which they are capable. For a child audience, they need to speak a little more slowly and distinctly than usual.

Ideally, an auditorium seating no more than 250 people is the maximum size for teen-age actors and child audiences. Larger theatres make it difficult for young actors to project subtle characterizations, and force them to exaggerate and to lose the effect of naturalness and honesty that they have developed in rehearsal. For these reasons, many theatre educators advocate a small room converted into an arena theatre seating perhaps 100 spectators. This room can be the exclusive domain of the drama group and be used for all rehearsals and performances. Students can decorate it to suit their tastes. They will not be obliged to give up their rehearsal space to other school activities, and they will develop a healthy group spirit.

On the other hand, civic groups are often handicapped because they cannot get into their rented theatre until the dress rehearsal period. Sometimes the theatre is so large that sound equipment must be used. In such cases, much dress rehearsal time must be spent in installing microphones and amplifiers and accustoming the actors to the system. One problem is that the actors' heels make noise that is picked up by the microphones. This can be overcome by using rugs on the stage floor, but the actors must rehearse on them to avoid accidents.

After the curtain on the last performance comes the clean-up, or strike, and a party. Energy and excitement from the whole experience of play production are so high at this point that it seems wise to capitalize on them by putting away the scenery, props, and costumes. The job can be done quickly if everyone stays and puts on work clothes. The strike should be planned by each crew head so that the workers know what is to be stored and what is to be discarded. The strike can be held the following week, but then it becomes a job instead of a labor of love. When the strike is held immediately after the last performance, actors begin to understand that theatre is more than standing in a spotlight and speaking lines; that it is a complicated group process, depending on back-stage people as much as on actors.

The strike takes a surprisingly short time to accomplish when many hands are ready to work. It should be followed by an informal party, on stage if possible, for the entire group. Producing a play develops a strong group spirit and a powerful sentimental attachment to the experience. A party helps to bring this spirit to a head and to ease the transition back to a normal schedule.

To make the whole experience a truly educational one, the director should call the entire group together for an evaluation about a week after the show. At this time a perceptive faculty member or townsman and the director can explain what they think were the strengths and weaknesses of the production; then, under a skillful leader, the group can take part in a discussion of what was most meaningful and least helpful. The director may also discover what kinds of plays the group is ready to give in the future. Perhaps, too, the enthusiasm developed by the play will lead to the formation of a drama group to serve as a nucleus for a continuous program of theatre activities. This evaluation session should be enlightening to an administrator or board member if he can be persuaded to attend. Needless to say, the tact and skill of the discussion leader are critical to the success of an evaluation period. His comments and the general form of the session should be carefully planned.

The theatre experience and its benefits are often either discounted or taken for granted, but they are too important to be neglected. Directors must point out achievements regularly and do it with loud trumpets. It is true that a satisfied audience is a great reward, but the effect of the experience on participating students is far more important. An enterprising director can solicit statements from other faculty members and from parents who notice subtle or obvious changes in students' behavior during and after producing a play. Concentration should improve, TV viewing should be more critical, and a cooperative, responsible attitude should be apparent. A young person working in a play will not be transformed overnight, but certain obvious results should be proclaimed.

Audience polls are useful in checking the effectiveness of a production. With the cooperation of home-room teachers, it is fairly easy to get evaluations from an audience of children. Ask each teacher to assign a one-page report covering such points as: "Who was your favorite character and why?" "What was your favorite moment in the play?" "What didn't you like about the play?" "What story would you like to see on the stage?" Sometimes children will draw pictures of the scenery and actors and surprise the director by their perception and imagination.

Polls of teen-age and adult audiences can be simple questionnaires filled out in the auditorium after the play. Questions should bring out reactions to the theme, the plot, the characters, the scenery, lighting, and costumes, and the dialogue and acting. The questionnaires can be signed or unsigned. If they are signed and addresses are given, the business manager has the beginnings of a good mailing list. If they are not to be signed, the answers may be a little more honest than they otherwise would be.

Information gathered from questionnaires, while not 100 percent accurate, can be useful for directors and play selection committees when planning future seasons.

One final question to be considered is the matter of drama critics. Should a critic come to the opening performance and publish a review? The answer should be yes, provided the critic is truly qualified. A student can write a good sports review and sometimes a good movie or book review because he knows the subject; but writing a theatre review requires highly sophisticated knowledge that includes dramatic laws and the director's and actors' tasks, the requirements of scenery and lighting, the relation of the play to other plays in theatre history, the playwright's intentions and methods, and the specific problems connected with the play in question. The critic should also know the philosophy of the theatre and director. Most newspaper critics do not bother to qualify themselves for the responsibility, but content themselves with clever or sarcastic remarks that do nothing to help the cast or director or crew improve their work. Such remarks can be devastating to beginning actors, especially if they are published the morning after opening night with two more performances to go. If a cast is demoralized by such criticism, the director should call the actors together and make them understand that the newspaper story is only one man's opinion.

He should point out the valid criticisms in the story and make a rebuttal to the invalid ones.

One solution to the problem of critics is to invite the neophyte critic to the theatre long before the performance and give him a tour of the facilities. At the same time he can be made aware of the group's purpose and philosophy in producing plays, its dependence on volunteers, its reasons for producing certain plays, and the differences between educational or civic theatre and professional theatre. With this background, the critic is able to write a knowledgeable review that is related to the intentions of the producing group. A well-written, thoughtful review is good publicity and can be instrumental in keeping standards high.

Fortunately, we in the amateur theatre have the advantage of not requiring a box-office success with every show. We can afford to experiment, to stretch our actors and audiences once in a while. The only thing we cannot afford to do is to rest on our laurels by repeating former successes. The theatre lives on new plays or new interpretations of old plays, and audiences depend on us for fresh entertainment and intellectual stimulation. This challenge will keep the living theatre alive and healthy as long as man continues to be a rational, imaginative being.

APPENDIX I

LAWYER LINCOLN

by

Betty Smith and Chase Webb
An American Historical Comedy

Reprinted by Permission of the Publishers Evanston, Row Peterson and Company, 1954. New York, Harper and Row. Boston, Walter H. Baker and Company. Rights to perform by permission of the publisher.

SCENE: *THE COMBINATION LIVING ROOM AND DINING ROOM OF SIS BEASELEY'S BOARDINGHOUSE IN A SMALL TOWN IN ILLINOIS.*
TIME: *THE SPRING OF THE YEAR, 1849.*
THE CURTAINS OPEN. SIS BEASELEY, *a comely, jolly woman of forty, is seated behind the table C, practicing from a "Missouri Harmony Book." She wears a dark gray dress with a tight-fitting waist and a full skirt which comes to her ankles. At the moment, there is a gingham apron over the dress. Her dark hair is parted in the middle and combed severely back on either side of her face into a knot at the nape of her neck.*

[UNIT ONE]

SIS. (*Singing in a high voice.*) "Oh, Thou in Whose Presence my soul takes delight." (*She isn't satisfied, stops singing, stands, comes around to left end of table, faces in the general direction of the*

135

fireplace, and tries the line again—an octave lower.) "Oh, Thou in Whose Presence my soul takes delight." (*A* FACE *peers in at the window* UC. SIS *becomes aware of it, shrieks, whirls, drops the song book, then runs toward window.* THE FACE *disappears.* SIS *calls out.*) Come in! Come in! Don't scare the life out of a body. (*She gets no answer, peers out curiously.*) Mr. Lincoln? Mr. Lincoln, is that you, sir, playin' another joke on me? Answer me! (*Still getting no response, she continues to peer through window. Her back is toward outside door* ULC; *and she doesn't see the door open slowly and her son,* NATE BEASELEY, *enter.* NATE, *a likeable, bashful young man of twenty-one, would be rather good-looking if he would only "slick" down his hair. He wears loose-fitting trousers, cowhide boots, and a homespun shirt open at the throat. A strap, worn diagonally across his back, over his shoulder and attached to two buttons on his pants, serves as a suspender. He slams door and grins.* SIS *jumps and turns to face him.*)

NATE.   Howdy, Maw! It's me.

SIS.   I declare, Nate Beaseley! Where on earth you been? Supper is over and gone, this good while. Jedge Davis et, and Lawyer Craig et. Seems like you could eat with the boarders, and not make me be a-doin' extra waitin' on you.

NATE.   (*Crosses to the chair behind the table C and sits.*) Lawyer Lincoln et yet?

SIS.   (*Crossing UR to kitchen door.*) He ain't come in yet, and Jedge Davis ain't likin' it. (*She exits into kitchen and returns almost immediately with a plate of food, which she carries to table and places in front of* NATE.) He's plumb worried . . . with court openin' first thing in the mornin' and not even the first man of the jury picked yet.

NATE.   Ain't hungry, Maw.

SIS.   You got to be hungry, after not eatin' dinner nor supper. (*Crosses up to sideboard, picks up knife, fork and spoon, brings them down and places them beside* NATE'S *plate.*) 'Pears like you got the love sickness or somethin'.

NATE.   (*In agony.*) All right! I'll eat, then. But don't be talkin' about such-like things. (*He starts to eat. There is a TAPPING on outside door ULC.* SIS *calls out.*)

SIS.   Some on in. (KEENIE JACKSON, *a lively, pretty girl of eighteen, enters ULC. She wears a very full-skirted and tight-waisted dress of red calico, black low-heeled strap pumps, and white stockings. Over her shoulders, she wears a short knitted shawl. Her black hair is combed off her face, pulled back behind her ears, and cascades down the back in curls and ringlets.*)

KEENIE.   Howdy, Miz Beaseley.

SIS.   Why, howdy, Keenie!

KEENIE.   (*Brightly.*) Evenin', Nate. (NATE *drops his head low over his plate and doesn't answer.* KEENIE *comes downstage to LC.*) Miz Beaseley . . . Maw said could we hold our Harmony Class over to your house tonight? Grandpaw's in a tantrum; and the singin' riles him up when he's that-a-way. So Maw can't have the class at our place.

SIS.   Mighty glad to have 'em. (*Crossing up behind Nate's chair.*) You tell your maw.

KEENIE.   Yes'm. (*She goes back to door ULC.* SIS *takes a step in her direction, stops, glances back at* NATE *and then to* KEENIE.)

SIS.   Anybody waitin' outside for to walk you home?

KEENIE.   No'm.

SIS.   (*Authoritatively.*) Nate!

NATE.   (*In agony.*) Aw, no, Maw.

KEENIE.   (*Tossing her head.*) I ain't a-needin' company.

SIS.   Any pretty girl needs company. Seems like you'll be pickin' you a husband soon.

KEENIE.   I ain't marryin' nobody less'n he can give me one of those new-style travelin' honeymoons.

NATE.   Ain't . . . nobody got money for such-like things.

KEENIE. Curly Allen's got . . . a little. (*Starts out, turns in doorway.*) I'll tell Maw, Miz Beaseley.

SIS. (*Going to right of doorway.*) And tell the ladies to bring along their own Missouri Harmony Book. I ain't got but the one.

KEENIE. Yes'm. (*Halfway out the door.*) I'll be right back (*provocatively*) . . . Nate! (*He shudders.* KEENIE *goes.* SIS *closes door, crosses down, and picks up her copy of the Missouri Harmony Book from the floor.*)

SIS. Why'n the world didn't you walk Keenie home?

NATE. 'Cause.

SIS. (*Crossing behind table to his left.*) Seems like you can't even talk in front of her no more. (*Puts book down, picks up* NATE'S *plate.*) Why, Nate Beaseley!

NATE. Ain't hungry.

SIS. Be it my cookin'?

NATE. No! Food ain't temptin' to me no more.

SIS. 'Taint your liver or stomach?

NATE. Not that I knows of.

SIS. Ain't you got no idea what it is?

NATE. Well . . . no . . .

SIS. The way you hesitate in answerin', son, makes me think you *do* have some notion why.

NATE. It ain't nothin' I can tell you. You wouldn't know my meanin'.

SIS. Prob'ly Mr. Lincoln would.

NATE. (*Jumping up.*) No, Maw! Not Mr. Lincoln. Don't tell him nothin's wrong with me. Don't you dast!

SIS. Shucks! He'll iron out your troubles in no time.

NATE. (*Grabbing the plate from her.*) Ain't nothin' troublin' me. See? (*Sits, starts gulping his food hastily.*) I'm eatin'!

SIS. (*Crossing behind him to* RC.) Must be somethin' powerful mean eff'n you don't want Mr. Lincoln to know.

NATE. Eff'n you won't go to Mr. Lincoln with it, I—I'll tell you. (*Reluctantly.*) It's . . . a gal.

SIS. It's Keenie!

NATE. 'Taint!

SIS. 'Tis.

NATE. Ain't thinkin' 'bout Keenie no more.

SIS. I reckon Curly Allen is.

NATE. And I reckon she'll marry him 'cause he's got the money for a travelin' honeymoon.

SIS. You got somethin' better'n money. Forty acres of good, black Illinoy land. All you need is enough git-up to ask her to marry you.

NATE. (*Jumping up again and going to door* ULC.) Ain't no use, Maw. (*Despairingly.*) She'll never marry me—Keenie won't. (*He pulls the door open desperately.* SIS *is alarmed.*)

SIS. What you aimin' to do, son?

NATE. Me? I'm just goin' out to slop the hogs.

[UNIT TWO]

(*He goes out, slamming the door behind him.* SIS *sighs, shakes her head, picks up Nate's plate and silverware, carries them to sideboard, and puts them down.* JUDGE DAVIS *and* LAWYER CRAIG *come down the stairs and enter at* L. JUDGE DAVIS *is a handsome, portly, distinguished-looking man, very much on his dignity. He has a ruddy face and a sonorous voice. He wears dark trousers, frock coat, white shirt with a stiff high collar—the points of which are turned down—and a black stock about his neck. A conspicuous-*

looking watch fob hangs from a pocket of his low-cut black vest.
LAWYER CRAIG *is thirty-five, pleasant-looking, with an agreeable
smile. Something of a dandy, he wears light-colored trousers, a
slightly darker coat, and possibly a flowered vest. There are frills
down the front of his white shirt, and he wears a flowing black
scarf tied into a bow for a tie. Both men come to LC and pause.)*

JUDGE.   Hasn't Mr. Lincoln come back yet?

SIS.   Don't you fret so, Jedge Davis. He's big enough and homely
enough to take care of hisself.

JUDGE.   Precisely! (*He crosses DR to fireplace and spreads his
coattails to warm his back.* CRAIG *crosses DL.*) What annoys us
is that he insists on taking care of *everyone else,* too. Eh, Craig?

CRAIG.   (*Nods.*) Anyone can get his ear. He delights in settling
things outside of court. Naturally, us lawyers lose the fees.

SIS.   (*Admiringly.*) Now, ain't that just like Mr. Lincoln!

JUDGE.   It's just like him to keep us waiting, too. (CRAIG *nods again,
sits in chair DL.*) Court starts tomorrow. We've got to get a jury
together. Mr. Lincoln must show more respect for his profession
—else I shall refuse to allow him on my circuit. He needs to be
taught a severe lesson! (*Fumes, looks at his watch.*) Confound
him! Why doesn't he ride in?

CRAIG.   He's probably down at the livery stable, swapping yarns. I
daresay he feels more at home with the horses than he does with
us.

JUDGE.   You trying to be facetious, Mr. Craig?

CRAIG.   (*respectfully.*) No, sir.

(LINCOLN *opens outside door ULC and enters. Forty years old
and clean-shaven, he wears a suit of rusty black—a little short and
tight in the breeches and sleeves and a trifle skimpy as to coattails.
His coarse hair is thick and unruly; and his white shirt collar rolls
over a clumsily knotted, thick, black bow tie. He wears a stovepipe hat in which he carries his legal papers. He closes the door,
comes LC, and removes his hat.)*

SIS. (*Beaming.*) Come in and set, Mr. Lincoln! (*Coming up stage right corner of table C.*) We were just talkin' of you.

LINCOLN. I plead guilty to whatever it was. (CRAIG *stands.*) That's the quickest way to settle a case, eh, Judge?

JUDGE. (*Moving to front of settee.*) We have no time for jokes, Mr. Lincoln. You are already very late.

LINCOLN. I stopped at the livery stable to . . .

CRAIG. (*Sauntering across to* JUDGE DAVIS.) So I was *not* being facetious, Judge.

LINCOLN. Seems like they gave me a mighty slow horse today. "You keep this horse for funerals, don't you?" I asked him. "Oh, no, sir," he answered. "Well, I'm glad of that," I said. "For if you did, you'd never get the corpse to the grave in time for the Resurrection." (SIS *laughs and moves around upstage of table.* CRAIG *smiles behind his hand, crosses below* JUDGE *and on to fireplace. The* JUDGE, *furious, strides to right end of bench in front of table C.*)

JUDGE. Mr. Lincoln, your conduct is inexcusable!

LINCOLN. Looks like I got to get right down to business, then. (*Removes some legal papers from inside of his hat.*) If you are ready (*holds out papers*) . . . I was able to pick up these briefs. (JUDGE DAVIS *takes papers, turns his back on* LINCOLN, *and begins leafing through the briefs.* SIS *leans across table and interjects quickly.*)

SIS. I had hoped, Mr. Lincoln, to get you talkin' about romance.

LINCOLN. (*Smiles, walks away toward chair DL.*) I'm afraid I'm no authority. My own romance ended rather abruptly.

SIS. (*Sympathetically; following him.*) Did the lady leave you?

LINCOLN. No. (*Sighs.*) She married me. (CRAIG *starts to guffaw; but* JUDGE DAVIS *frowns at him, and he quickly subsides.*)

JUDGE. (*Rattling the papers.*) If you please, Mr. Lincoln!

LINCOLN. Just a moment, Judge. The law will always wait. But romance is a mighty fleeting thing. (*Bows slightly.*) I am at your service, Mrs. Beaseley.

SIS.   Could you advise on how a feller could get hisself up to the altar?

LINCOLN.   My advice would be purely theoretical. I shied twice—myself—before they got the halter on me. However, an attractive woman like you . . .

SIS.   (*Turns away, walks to left end of bench in front of table C.*) Oh, it's nothin' personal. It's my boy, Nate. (*Sits, faces* LINCOLN.) He can't raise enough gumption to ask Miz Jackson's Keenie to marry him because he ain't got the money for the travelin' honeymoon Keenie reckons she's got to have. You got any ideas, Mr. Lincoln?

LINCOLN.   (*Sits DL, stretches his legs.*) No. But Mrs. Lincoln might. If I only had time to consult her.

SIS.   Time is what we ain't got—with Curly Allen a-courtin' her while Nate's settin' around.

JUDGE.   (*Sarcastically.*) Indeed, Mr. Lincoln has time. (*Pacing to front of settee.*) My time! His clients' time. The state's time. He may waste all of it. (*Bitterly; turning and glaring at* LINCOLN.) It doesn't belong to him.

LINCOLN.   Man back in Indiana, going to be hanged, felt the same way. He was being taken to the scaffold in a slow-moving cart. A lot of folks were running ahead to get a place where they could have a good view. As one bunch of perspiring men rushed past the cart, the condemned man called out: "What's your hurry, boys? You got plenty of time. There won't be any fun till I get there."

JUDGE.   Bah!

LINCOLN.   (*Stands.*) Judge, here is an opportunity to repay Mrs. Beaseley for being so kind to us. (*Crossing to C.*) Let me make a bargain with you. If I succeed in getting Nate to propose, you are never to lecture me again about wasting time. If I fail—

JUDGE.   (*Eagerly.*) If you fail—?

LINCOLN.   (*Moving to left end of settee.*) I swear I'll give up what you call wasting time and devote all of it to you, my clients, and my state.

JUDGE.   You promise that? If you fail?

LINCOLN.   I do!

JUDGE.   It's a bargain.

LINCOLN.   Good.

[UNIT THREE]

LINCOLN.   (*Turns to* SIS.) Mrs. Beaseley, how old is Nate?

SIS.   He just turned the corner on twenty-one.

LINCOLN.   No!

SIS.   Yes! It was livin' down-country with his Paw so long made him kinda slow-like. (NATE *enters from outside door ULC, a bucket in his hand.*)

LINCOLN.   Twenty-one! I think I see a way to—! (*Sees* NATE.) Nate? (NATE *closes door, turns, looks at the others curiously, comes downstage two or three steps.* LINCOLN *addresses the* JUDGE *smilingly.*) Judge Davis, I see how I can waste my time and still 'tend strictly to business. I have already found our first juror for court tomorrow!

JUDGE.   (*Annoyed.*) Really, Mr. Lincoln—!

CRAIG.   (*Walking upstage.*) A juror? Who?

LINCOLN.   Nate Beaseley! (NATE *drops the bucket.*)

LINCOLN.   Why not? He's qualified. He's twenty-one. (*Crossing to* NATE, *meeting him at LC.*) How'd you like to be a juror, Nate, and earn yourself some money for . . . say . . . a traveling honeymoon?

NATE.   (*Gulping in his eagerness.*) I'd admire to do it, Mr. Lincoln! I'll be a first rate juror. I'll make 'em bring in whatever verdict you tell me.

LINCOLN.   We could use eleven more like him, eh, Judge? (*Puts on his hat, goes ULC to door.*) I'll go tell Miss Keenie you've got something mighty important to tell her, Nate.

NATE.   I'll sure be able to pop the question now.

LINCOLN.   Judge, I consider my case as good as won. (*The* JUDGE *beckons to* CRAIG, *who moves downstage and joins him near fireplace.*)

CRAIG.   The *girl* is still to be reckoned with, Abe.

SIS.   (*Stands.*) Oh, she'll grab him, all right. (*Goes upstage to right of outside door ULC.*) Mr. Lincoln, don't trouble yourself a-fetchin' her. Keenie's on her way over here now with the Harmony Class. (JUDGE DAVIS *and* CRAIG *converse in whispers.*)

LINCOLN.   I want to talk to her alone—and sort of smooth the way for Nate. (*He exits ULC.* SIS *closes the door.*)

SIS.   I just got time to set my bread to rizin' 'fore they get here. (*Crossing UR toward kitchen door.*) Talk to the Jedge and Lawyer Craig, boy. (*The two older men come out of their whispered huddle as they hear their names.*) And tell 'em thankee for lettin' you be a juror. (*She goes out into kitchen. The men eye* NATE *speculatively.*)

NATE.   (*At LC; gulps.*) Thankee.

CRAIG.   (*Advancing to front of settee.*) Just what do you think a juryman does, Nate? (*Exchanges a wink with the* JUDGE.)

NATE.   (*Crosses C, to front of bench.*) He listens to both sides tell the criminal what he done. Then he listens while the jedge tells the lawyers what they just done said. Then he goes into a little room with the other jurors and swaps stories till the jedge is fit to be tied. Then they come out and say, "Guilty," or "Not Guilty" . . . 'cordin' to how feelin' is in the town.

JUDGE.   Why do they do this?

NATE.   'Cause they git paid for it.

CRAIG.   You'll do. (*He returns to fireplace, as he and the* JUDGE *ex-*

change a nod which is unseen by NATE. *The* JUDGE *clears his throat.*)

JUDGE. There is . . . ah . . . one thing . . . ah . . . Mr. Lincoln didn't make plain. (*Takes a step toward* NATE; *sternly.*) As a juror, you are not permitted to *talk* to anyone.

NATE. (*Surprised.*) Not—nobody?

CRAIG. If you so much as say "Howdy" to anyone, you're disqualified.

NATE. "Dis . . . dis. . . ?" What does that mean?

JUDGE. It means you won't get the money for that honeymoon of yours.

CRAIG. That's right.

NATE. Gosh! (*Visibly worried.*) Then, Keenie 'n' me . . . I can't . . .

JUDGE. (*Impressively.*) Talking to the ladies is especially forbidden. They don't keep secrets.

NATE. (*Scratching his head.*) Eff'n I talk, I don't git the *money* for the honeymoon. Eff'n I *don't* talk, I don't git the honeymoon. (*Baffled.*) Gosh . . .

JUDGE. I will now swear you in as a juror. After that, you're not allowed to say a word until court session is over.

CRAIG. Except, of course, to your fellow jurymen.

JUDGE. (*Holding up his hand.*) I hereby pronounce you a juror. You understand? (NATE *nods affirmatively and gulps, afraid to speak. From off UR, the sound of LADIES' VOICES can be heard, as they approach the outside door ULC.* NATE *turns, looks at the door apprehensively, runs to his bucket, picks it up, and then bolts off into the kitchen UR.* JUDGE DAVIS *and* LAWYER CRAIG *laugh.*) I guess I put a fine crimp into Mr. Lincoln's plans. The boy is nothing if not conscientious. He'll keep silent all week! Lincoln will never get a proposal out of him now!

CRAIG. You're mighty shrewd, Judge. (*Sobering.*) But somehow, I think that Abe will win out. I'd be willing to wager that . . .

[UNIT FOUR]

(The door ULC is thrown open; and LULY MAY, *a plump pretty girl of seventeen—always giggling—enters, followed by Keenie's mother,* MRS. JACKSON, *who is tall, large, good-natured, but quite the bossy type. Following her is* MISS SOPHRONY, *a spare, eager, man-hunting spinster.* ABE LINCOLN *and* KEENIE *come in last. The ladies—with the exception of* LULY MAY *and* KEENIE—*wear bonnets, heavy shawls, long dresses of coarse materials and deeper colors. The clothes of the younger women are of more fashionable materials in gayer colors. All of them carry their Missouri Harmony Books. As they crowd through doorway ULC,* JUDGE DAVIS *and* CRAIG *look at each other in alarm, then dash across toward stairway at L in a belated attempt to escape the ladies. They are about to disappear upstairs when* LINCOLN *stops them.)*

LINCOLN.   Gentlemen! Gentlemen! (*Removes his hat.*) The ladies have arrived! (MISS SOPHRONY *simpers and tosses her head, eyeing the portly judge avidly.* LULY MAY *squirms and giggles on a high note.* CRAIG *and* JUDGE DAVIS *look at each other, sigh, shake their heads, and shrug in defeat.* MRS. JACKSON *crosses to them and vigorously shakes hands with each.*)

MRS. JACKSON.   Howdy! I'm Miz Jackson, Keenie's maw. (SIS *hurries in from kitchen UR, wiping flour off her arms, and comes downstage to right end of bench in front of table C.*)

SIS.   Howdy, gals. Here I be—all over flour! (*Indicating the men.*) Let me make you acquainted with Jedge Davis and Lawyer Craig. (*They bow gallantly, murmur politely.*) They're boardin' with me while court's in session. (*Indicating* MRS. JACKSON.) You all know Keenie's maw. (MRS. JACKSON *makes a little bob of her head.*) This here's Miss Sophrony.

MISS SOPHRONY.   (*Eagerly; as the men again murmur politely.*) Married?

CRAIG.   Absolutely! For the second time.

JUDGE.   (*Hurriedly.*) And *I'm* engaged to a very jealous widow.

(*He pulls out his handkerchief and wipes his face.* MISS SOPHRONY *registers disappointment.*)

MISS SOPHRONY. Shucks!

SIS. (*As* LULY MAY *approaches the men.*) And here's Luly May, Keenie's particular gal friend. (LULY MAY *giggles.* CRAIG *stretches out his hand. She is just about to take it, then she abruptly changes her mind, draws her hand back in quick retreat, giggles louder, conceals her face in her hands, runs across to right of* SIS, *and hides behind the older woman.* CRAIG *and* JUDGE DAVIS *exchange sour looks.*)

LINCOLN. (*Ushering* KEENIE *downstage.*) Miss Keenie! (*She makes a curtsey. The men bow.* SIS *starts toward kitchen door UR.*)

SIS. The parlor's (*with an indicative gesture off UR*) waitin' on you if you don't mind traipsin' through the kitchen.

MISS SOPHRONY. (*Muttering, as she crosses UR and exits.*) Land o' Goshen! The best ones are always took.

MRS. JACKSON (*Hopefully; to the men.*) Will you gentlemen join us in a little close harmony? (JUDGE DAVIS *and* LAWYER CRAIG *begin elbowing each other out of the way in their efforts to get through doorway L and upstairs.*)

JUDGE. Sorry! I have some—briefs to study.

CRAIG. Important letters to write home. (*They have escaped.* LULY MAY *giggles, runs UR and out through kitchen door.* SIS *picks up her "Missouri Harmony Book" from the table.*)

LINCOLN. I'd like a word with Miss Keenie. Alone.

MRS. JACKSON. Certainly, Mr. Lincoln. (*She also crosses UR and goes out into kitchen.* LINCOLN *guides* KEENIE *across to front of settee, where she sits.* SIS *hovers uncertainly UR.* LINCOLN *puts his hat on right end of table C.*)

LINCOLN. Send Nate in here, will you, Mrs. Beaseley?

SIS. Yes, sir. (*She exits to kitchen.* LINCOLN *stands at left end of settee, looking down at* KEENIE.)

[UNIT FIVE]

KEENIE.   Like I was sayin', Mr. Lincoln, I'm willin' to give Nate a chance. But I won't marry no man as couldn't even ask me.

LINCOLN.   (*Gently.*) Not even when he worships you? (*There is a pause. The VOICES of the Harmony Class drift in faintly from off R in the parlor. The Ladies are practicing "Old Salem," singing in harmony: "Do-do-re-mi-do-re-do-me-re-do-ti," etc. The song continues softly under the dialogue.*)

KEENIE.   It's silly of him not to even look at me. (*Tosses her head.*) Curly Allen looks, and he sure does talk. I reckon he's fonder of me.

LINCOLN.   You'll find Nate very talkative, now, I think. (NATE *appears UR and hesitates uncertainly near doorway.* LINCOLN *sees him, crosses upstage, takes the boy's arm, leads him down to right of settee, near fireplace.*) Come in. Come in, Nate. I was just about to go. (*Crosses ULC to outside door.*) I think I'll just sit out on the porch in the moonlight and enjoy the singing. (*To* KEENIE; *as he opens door.*) Call me if you need any help. (*He goes out ULC and closes door. There is another pause. The singing, "Sol-la-ti-mi-re-do-sol-fa-mi-re-mi," etc., can be heard more clearly in the distance.* KEENIE *pats the seat at her right.*)

KEENIE.   Set down, Nate. (*He does so.*) It's a mighty pretty evenin'. (*He looks at her dumbly.*) Mr. Lincoln said you had somethin' to say to me. (*He turns away bashfully.*) Was it about the cotillion? (*Waits, gets no answer, pleats her dress coyly.*) 'Cause, eff'n it is, I already passed my promise to go with Curly Allen. (NATE *looks at her, anguished; but he presses his lips tightly together.*) I could change my mind, though. (*Impatiently.*) Well, Nate? (*Rises.*) Well? Well! (*Beginning to shout, stamps angrily away to front of bench C.*) Am I so all-fired ugly you can't even speak to me? (NATE *presses his lips determinedly together and makes some mumbling sounds. She turns and shakes her finger at him.*) Very well! Curly ain't so backward, I must say. I guess I better start givin' him a mite more encouragement. (*In despair,* NATE *gets up and lunges UR toward kitchen door. Terrified,* KEENIE *runs to out-*

side door ULC and calls out.) Mr. Lincoln! Mr. Lincoln! (LIN-COLN *comes hurrying in ULC.* NATE *is about to escape through the kitchen door.*)

[UNIT SIX]

LINCOLN.   Nate! (NATE *stops.*) Haven't you proposed to Keenie yet? (NATE *shakes his head negatively.* LINCOLN *smiles genially.*) Oh, well. That's a mere technicality. As I recall, I didn't do any proposing either; and here I am, a married man. (*Crosses RC, midway between* NATE *and* KEENIE.) So if you two will just take it for granted, I believe we can announce. . . . (NATE *shakes his head eagerly, affirmatively.* KEENIE *stamps her foot stubbornly.*

KEENIE.   No!

LINCOLN.   Nate loves you.

KEENIE.   Ain't enough. (*Stamps her foot again.*) I ain't takin' no man less'n he can make me a first-rate, bang-up proposal!

LINCOLN.   (*Puts his hand encouragingly on* NATE'S *arm.*) Go ahead, Nate. (NATE *shakes his head stubbornly.*) You want to marry her? (NATE *shakes his head eagerly, indicating an affirmative.* LINCOLN *ushers him downstage to front of fireplace.*) Ask her, then. (NATE *shakes his head negatively.* KEENIE *waits hopefully.*)

KEENIE.   (*Pleadingly.*) You got to ask me proper, or it'll get around that *I* done the proposin'. (NATE *sighs, shakes his head very sadly. She folds her arms and turns her back on him.*) All right! Don't!

LINCOLN.   Just try it, Nate. Keenie'll meet you more than halfway, I'm sure. (*She tosses her head, but looks around slyly to see if* NATE'S *going to use the suggestion.* NATE, *in stubborn but agonized pantomime, indicates "No."* LINCOLN *sighs.*) Well, I guess there's no hope for it. You won't propose, and she won't have you unless you do. I might as well give up. At least the Judge will be pleased. (*He turns to go. Frantically,* NATE *grabs him by the coattails and detains him.* LINCOLN *stops and stares at* NATE. *The youth looks at him with such dumb pleading that* LINCOLN *decides to try again.*) I reckon I've got to do the proposing, then. (NATE *seems delighted.* LINCOLN *moves to left of* NATE, *takes his arm, and they both cross to right of* KEENIE *in front of bench.*) Miss Keenie . . . I ain't much on sweet talking. But I love you down deep, and I got a good farm that will take care of us in our old age.

KEENIE. (*Pertly.*) But I ain't old yet.

LINCOLN. Maybe Curly Allen's got a fancy way of speaking, but (*at the mention of* CURLY, NATE *clenches his fist, frowns, and almost growls*) . . . he can't care for you like I do. (NATE *"fetches up" a deep sigh.*) No man could, Keenie, if you won't have me, I'm like to die. (NATE *looks very woebegone.*) Say you'll have me! (NATE *hopefully holds out his hands toward her.*)

KEENIE. No. Nate's got to ask me, and I got to have the travelin' honeymoon.

LINCOLN. The honeymoon is assured. Nate will have money. He's going to serve on the—! (NATE *stops him, tugging desperately at* LINCOLN'S *sleeve and shaking his head violently, entreating in pantomime that the lawyer must say no more.*) Of course you'll have the money. The Judge and I—! (*Afraid that* LINCOLN *will reveal that he is to be a juror,* NATE *tries to put his hand over* LINCOLN'S *mouth.* KEENIE *observes this and is furious.*)

KEENIE. See! See! He's got the money, but he ain't wantin' me to know. (*Paces irately away to far DL.*) I ain't never a-goin' to marry him now. Never!

LINCOLN. Nate! For the last time! Will you propose to her? (NATE *shakes his head pitifully, points to his sealed lips.* LINCOLN *walks across to* KEENIE.) Miss Keenie! For the last time! Will you have him without the words? (*She folds her arms, shakes her head stubbornly.* LINCOLN *sighs, shrugs, and turns away up to LC.*) I guess I'm licked . . . as I said to the man who tried to shoot me. (*Hesitates, his face breaking into a faint smile.*) Back in Little Pigeon Creek, one of the ugliest men I ever did see pushed a big pistol into my face and said he was going to kill me. "Why?" I asked him. . . . "Well," he said, "some years ago I swore an oath that if I ever came across an uglier man than myself, I'd shoot him on the spot." . . . (*Chuckles.*) "Stranger," I said, "shoot me! For if I'm uglier than you, I don't want to live." (*Starts toward stairway.*) I bid you good night.

KEENIE.   Mr. Lincoln! (*She runs up behind him, grabs his coattails, pulls him back to LC, pushes him toward* NATE, *and waits anxiously for Lincoln to resume negotiations.* LINCOLN *scratches his head, perplexed. He looks from* KEENIE *to* NATE.)

LINCOLN.   There must be some way out of this. Let me see . . . (*He looks again at* NATE, *who turns his back toward* LINCOLN. *He glances toward* KEENIE *a moment; then he straightens up, as though he had come to a decision.* KEENIE *moves slightly toward DL again;* LINCOLN *crosses, stands next to* KEENIE, *and begins to speak for her as he addresses* NATE.) Nate . . . I'm kind of a pretty gal, and there are heaps o' men willing to marry me. But somehow, I hanker after you. (KEENIE *is indignant. She pulls his coat, frowns, and shakes her head negatively. The SINGING off R in the parlor HAS STOPPED now.* LINCOLN *tries again.*) Nate . . . I know you ain't much on talking. Maybe I admire you for it in my secret heart. I know that—like most men—you're trying to duck the yoke of matrimony. (*Sighs, turns away, speaks as to himself.*) And I don't blame you. (*He takes his coat lapels in his hands, assumes a legal mien, and begins tramping up and downstage in the LC area—as though addressing an imaginary jury.*) Courtship is the long-drawn-out trial which usually leads to the passing of the life sentence—marriage. (*Indicating* KEENIE *with a sweep of his hand.*) The plaintiff in this case is the woman. She is fighting for her inalienable rights: a pretty proposal, vows of undying love, and a traveling honeymoon. (*Indicates* NATE.) On the other hand, the man—the defendant—has his rights also, the most important of which is the right to his liberty! (*He holds up his hand, as if to stem either protest or applause from spectators in his imaginary courtroom.*) It may be said that the plaintiff is fighting for her birthrights . . . and that the defendant is fighting for his rights.

KEENIE.   (*Trying to recall him to the practical matter at hand.*) Pst! Pst!

LINCOLN.   The plaintiff is entitled to her demands. The defendant, on the other hand, is entitled to hold out on the plaintiff. My sympathies are with the young woman. Yet, I cannot but feel that there is much to be said for the defendant. (NATE *crosses to* LINCOLN, *jerks his coat sleeve, nudges him, points to* KEENIE *and to himself. When* KEENIE *sees that* LINCOLN'S *attention has been recalled to the matter of the moment, she turns her back on the men.* LINCOLN *takes a different tone.*) Oh—yes! What was I saying? (*Returns to* KEENIE'S *side.*) Yes, Nate, it would be mighty convenient if you could say pretty things to me now and then. But if you can't, you just can't. And that's all. So I got to take you like you are and love you for the things you're lacking in. (NATE *is highly pleased. He steps over, shakes* LINCOLN'S *hand sincerely, and then returns to his side of the room—at left end of settee.*) I know you're a good boy and a hard worker and mighty sweet to your Maw. (NATE, *pleased but bashful, draws circles on the floor with his foot.* KEENIE *stands rigid.*) And when you're slicked up proper, you're almost good-looking. (NATE *is almost overcome by this praise.* KEENIE'S *shoulders shake with suppressed laughter.* NATE *beckons to* LINCOLN, *catches the lawyer's attention, attempts to express something in pantomime. He holds his hand about a foot from the floor, then raises it to about a foot and a half. He points to* KEENIE. LINCOLN *is puzzled, scratches his head.*) How's that? (*In pantomime,* NATE *holds something gingerly in his arms. He pantomimes dropping it. It breaks; he grieves.* LINCOLN *guesses.*) Oh! Eggs! (NATE *nods eagerly, again holds his hand about a foot from the floor.*) And—chickens! (NATE *continues to nod.* LINCOLN *turns to* KEENIE.) When we're married, I'm going to buy you a chicken. You can sell the eggs it lays. And when you get enough money (NATE *holds his hand about two feet above the floor*) . . . you can buy a bigger chicken.

KEENIE.   (*Stamps her foot in rage, shakes her fist at the men.*) Oh, you will, will you? Chickens! I guess you'd even let me clean out the coops eff'n it'd make me happy. (NATE *nods blissfully.*) Oh, you—! You—! You got the worse case of "no-gumption" I ever did see. (*Wrathfully.*) Nate Beaseley, I wouldn't marry you now eff'n I had to die an old maid! I hate you! I hate you! You horrible . . .

LINCOLN.   (*Breaking in on her tirade.*) Ain't she pretty when she's in a temper? (*Firmly.*) Now, Keenie, stop acting-up and come over here and kiss me like you should. (KEENIE *doesn't quite know how to take this. She stamps her foot, scowls, and lowers her head. After a moment, she looks up at* LINCOLN *and smiles demurely.*)

KEENIE.   Don't . . . mind . . . eff'n I do. (*She holds out her arms and starts toward* LINCOLN. *He holds out his arms and goes to meet her.* NATE *looks on, open-mouthed with astonishment as* LINCOLN *and* KEENIE *meet just below left end of bench in front of table C.* LINCOLN *puts his arms about* KEENIE *and is just on the point of kissing her when* NATE *comes suddenly to his senses.*)

[UNIT SEVEN]

NATE.   Hold on, Mr. Lincoln! Hold on! (*Crossing to him.*) You're just speakin' up for me—not actin' for me! (*He yanks* KEENIE *away from* LINCOLN *and takes her in his arms for a long embrace.* KEENIE *seems delighted.* LINCOLN *counters to right of* NATE, *watches the couple ruefully for a moment.*)

LINCOLN.   I'm like the old lady who baked the pies and never even got to taste them.

NATE.   (*Suddenly howls.*) I spoke out! (*Pushes* KEENIE *away from him, turns accusingly to* LINCOLN.) You done tempted me! (*Despairingly; pointing to the surprised* KEENIE.) And she done made me break the law! Now I don't get to be no juryman, and I lose the money for the travelin' honeymoon!

LINCOLN.   What's this?

NATE.   Jedge Davis swore me in and said I dasn't speak to *nobody!*

LINCOLN.   (*Glances toward stairs, smiles grimly.*) And that's why you wouldn't speak out and propose? (NATE *nods.*) I see now what the Judge was up to. (*Puts his hand on* NATE'S *shoulder.*) It's only during the trial, Nate, that you can't talk to outsiders.

NATE.   You mean—it's all right, then? (LINCOLN *nods.* NATE *emits an enormous sigh of relief, goes to* KEENIE, *grins happily.*) Well

. . . you done won me, Keenie. (KEENIE *pouts, but* NATE *very masterfully takes her into his arms and kisses her.* LINCOLN *hurries UR to kitchen door and calls out.*)

LINCOLN. (*Loudly.*) Mrs. Beaseley! Mrs. Jackson! Ladies! (*Turns and strides across to L, calls upstairs.*) Come on down, Judge Davis! You, too, Mr. Craig! I want to show you something! (*Almost instantly,* JUDGE DAVIS *and* LAWYER CRAIG *come down the stairs and appear at L.* LINCOLN *laughs accusingly.*) Eavesdroppers!

CRAIG. I told you he'd do it, Judge.

LINCOLN. And in spite of you.

JUDGE. Humph!

LINCOLN. You promised if I won, you wouldn't lecture me again.

JUDGE. Nevertheless, Mr. Lincoln—

LINCOLN. You got to keep your promise now, Judge Davis. (MRS. JACKSON, LULY MAY, SIS BEASELEY, *and* MISS SOPHRONY *crowd excitedly in through kitchen door UR. They see* KEENIE, *still locked in* NATE'S *embrace.* MRS. JACKSON *hurries directly downstage to fireplace, hoping to get a better look.*)

[UNIT EIGHT]

MRS. JACKSON. Keenie done landed him!

SIS. My boy! (*Begins to sob, advances to right end of bench.*) I'm so . . . so . . . hap-hap-happy!

(LULY MAY *giggles loudly.* NATE *and* KEENIE *separate in confusion.* NATE *remains awkwardly but happily at LC.* KEENIE *moves to front of bench C.* MISS SOPHRONY *sighs blissfully as she and* LULY MAY *rush to* KEENIE *and kiss her profusely on the cheek.* MISS SOPHRONY *is at right of* KEENIE; LULY MAY *is at her left.* MRS. JACKSON *hurries across to* KEENIE; *and the others make room for her and* SIS—*both of whom fairly smother* KEENIE *with kisses of joy.* LINCOLN *and* CRAIG *move down to* NATE—LINCOLN *at the boy's right—and both shake* NATE'S *hand in congratulations. The* JUDGE *merely moves down to chair DL and watches sulkily.*)

MISS SOPHRONY. Be you married, Mr. Lincoln?

LINCOLN. (*Sighs deeply.*) Yes.

MISS SOPHRONY. (*Also sighing deeply.*) Too bad!

LINCOLN. (*Looks at her, shudders slightly.*) Well—*sometimes* I'm almost reconciled!

SIS. We got you to thank for this, Mr. Lincoln.

MRS. JACKSON. Yes, indeedy! (LULY MAY *giggles again.*)

CRAIG. Abe, have you any advice to offer these young people who are about to embark on what is commonly called "the sea of matrimony"?

LINCOLN. I have one rule for a happy marriage. (NATE *moves in close to* LINCOLN'S *left;* KEENIE *comes to his right.* LINCOLN *puts an arm about the shoulder of each.*) My wife explained it to me on our wedding day.

CRAIG. If I may inquire—?

LINCOLN. We agreed that she settle all minor problems and I settle all the major problems.

CRAIG. Does it work?

LINCOLN. Perfectly. (*After a pause.*) So far, we don't seem to have had any *major* problems. (*Shaking* NATE'S *hand again.*) Leave everything to your wife, son, if you want a happy marriage.

NATE. (*Nervously.*) What does a feller say when he faces the preacher?

LINCOLN. I said, "With this ring I now thee wed, and with all my worldly goods I thee endow."

JUDGE. (*Sourly.*) Good gracious, Lincoln! The statute fixes all that.

LINCOLN. I know. I just thought I'd add a little dignity to the statute. Now! (*Claps his hands, stamps his feet.*) How about a song for the happy pair? (*In a nasal, toneless, but somehow pleasant-sounding voice,* LINCOLN *starts singing, "Hop, Blue Jay."*) "Old Blue Jay is hoppin', eatin' seeds you're droppin'."

MISS SOPHRONY.   (*As* LULY MAY *giggles.*) No, no, Mr. Lincoln. (*Takes pitch pipe from her reticule, sounds the first note, nods to* SIS.) Like this!

SIS.   (*Singing.*) "Old Blue Jay is hoppin', eatin' seeds you're droppin'."

MRS. JACKSON.   (*Joining her on second line.*) "Your corn will never grow."

KEENIE.   (*Coming in on third line.*) "Old Blue Jay is merry."

LULY MAY.   "Eats all he can carry."

LADIES.   (*All together.*) "Hoppin' down the road." (LINCOLN, *in his zeal to join in, jumps at the next phrase before the ladies are ready and sings it out alone.*)

LINCOLN.   "Hop, Blue Jay!" (LULY MAY *has a fit of giggling and has to stop singing.* LINCOLN *and the* LADIES *sing together.*) "Here's a clod for you! Hop, Blue Jay. Eatin' time is through." (*During the last line,* LINCOLN *motions* CRAIG *and the* JUDGE *to join in. They look at each other uncertainly.* LINCOLN *takes* SIS BEASELEY'S *hand, and they stand in dance position.* KEENIE *grabs* NATE'S *hand; and they—with* LINCOLN *and* SIS—*form a square and start to dance. All, with the exception of the* JUDGE—*who continues to sulk—sing the second verse. As the music gets under way,* CRAIG *takes* LULY MAY'S *hand; and they join in the dance.* MISS SOPHRONY *leads the singing.* MRS. JACKSON *stands near the* JUDGE, *glaring angrily at him and waiting for him to invite her to dance.*)

ALL.   (*Singing and dancing.*) "Old Blue Jay is floppin'; now no more he's hoppin', My corn is sure to grow.

> Old Blue Jay's a smarty. But this ain't no party;
> Old Blue Jay must go!
> Flop, Blue Jay. Go on, flop away.
> Flop, Blue Jay; this is not your day."

(*Near the end of the song,* SIS BEASELEY—*panting heavily—slips out of the dance, sinks down onto the settee, and sits fanning her-*

self with her apron. With a grotesque but somehow gallant gesture, LINCOLN *offers his arm to* MISS SOPHRONY, *who is practically overcome with delight. He takes her aside from the other dancers, and they are soon off in a bouncing polka. With the exception of* LINCOLN *and* MISS SOPHRONY, *all start singing the second verse again.*)

LINCOLN. (*Calling out over the music.*) This is how it should be danced.

MISS SOPHRONY. (*Proudly.*) You gals better shine up to Mr. Lincoln for the cotillion in the Jedge's honor. He's a mighty fine dancer! (KEENIE *and* NATE *stop dancing to watch, as do the others.*)

KEENIE. (*Smiles provocatively at* LINCOLN.) I wouldn't say "No" eff'n Mr. Lincoln was to ask *me* to dance a set with him!

LINCOLN. (*Stops dancing.*) Miss Keenie, if I may have the honor—

NATE. (*Shouting out.*) No, you don't, Mr. Lincoln! (*He grabs* KEENIE'S *hand possessively, leads her ULC and through outside door. She goes—with a backward, smiling glance at* LINCOLN. LULY MAY *giggles.* SIS *suddenly claps her hands for attention.*)

SIS. Ladies! Ladies! We must get on with our practicin'. (*Leads the way upstage and stands near kitchen door while* LULY MAY, MISS SOPHRONY, *and* MRS. JACKSON *cross UR and file off.* SIS *speaks invitingly to* JUDGE DAVIS, *who has remained at DL.*) Jedge, we'd be mighty honored if you'd join us. And you, Mr. Lincoln and Mr. Craig.

LINCOLN. (*Upstage of table C.*) Why not, Judge?

CRAIG. Yes. (*Prepares to follow the* LADIES *out UR.*) Why not?

JUDGE. Perhaps I will.

SIS. Come along, then.

JUDGE. Presently, Mrs. Beaseley. (SIS *and* CRAIG *exit to kitchen.* LINCOLN *starts to follow them.* JUDGE DAVIS *clears his throat significantly.* LINCOLN, *his attention caught, turns and waits curiously. The* JUDGE *crosses to him.*) Mr. Lincoln . . . I couldn't help eavesdropping. And I grudgingly admit that I admire the way you handled that proposal.

LINCOLN.   Then I'm not to be lectured any more for skylarking?

JUDGE.   I'll never say another critical word (*lowers his voice confidentially*) . . . providing you do something for me.

LINCOLN.   Name it. (JUDGE DAVIS *looks around cautiously, takes* LINCOLN *by the arm and draws him away from kitchen door to RC.*)

JUDGE.   A very wealthy but extremely jealous widow back in Springfield happens to be interested in me, and . . .

LINCOLN.   (*Rubbing his hands together.*) And you want me to win this lady for you?

JUDGE.   (*Wiping his brow.*) Gad, *no*, Mr. Lincoln! I want you to get rid of her for me!

(The CURTAINS CLOSE quickly.)

NOTES ON PRODUCING THE PLAY

(From the published play script)

One of the most appealing aspects of *Lawyer Lincoln* is that it has sufficient *worth* to warrant an "all-out" production—in terms of casting, directing, costuming, and staging. Fortunately, it is one of those literary and stageworthy works which makes any degree of effort and ingenuity seem "worth it." *Lawyer Lincoln* is by no means a "holiday" play; its subject matter, its situation, and its theme are timeless and universal. Unlike most *Lincoln* plays, there are a number of *other* important roles; so the success of the presentation does not have to hinge completely on exceptional casting of the title-character.

As publishers, we naturally feel that *Lawyer Lincoln* deserves to be played in as wide a variety of circumstances as possible. To that end, we offer the following general suggestions:

While the stairway at Left affords several useful and attractive playing levels, the fact that no set of steps is available—especially in assembly and contest work—will detract but little. A door, or even a simple opening in the cyclorama, will prove adequate for the requirements of this particular acting edition. . . . The costume suggestions, enumerated on the character's first appearance, can be varied in an unlimited number of ways. Certainly, no attempt at *authentic costuming* should be insisted upon. The costume room or attic trunks will undoubtedly yield old dresses and suits which—while not necessarily coinciding with the period of the play—can easily be altered slightly to serve this play's purpose. Lincoln's stovepipe hat is a kind of trademark, of course; but the audience will soon accept the character without it. The costumes for Keenie and Luly May should be somewhat more colorful and "dressy" than those of the older women. . . . Since the play is a comedy, the lighting should be both warm and fairly general. Although the present script suggests the two *chief* light sources as being the lamp and the fireplace glow, these would need to be "boosted" appreciably in order that the facial expressions of the actors (and Nate's extensive pantomiming particularly) not be lost by the audience.

OPTIONAL ENDING

While it will be almost immediately apparent that the music and dancing add a desirable flavor and "life" to the play's climax, there are sure to be a number of producing groups that will find it necessary to omit it. The time limitations imposed by many one-act play tournaments will prompt certain directors to eliminate it. Other directors, either because of a limited rehearsal schedule or a feeling of inadequacy with reference to music and dance, may tend to reject producing *Lawyer Lincoln* because it is "too difficult."

To anticipate and offset such objection, we take the position that since the singing and dancing are more in the nature of the *celebration* of the climax (Nate's and Keenie's engagement) than a part of the actual climax *itself,* the singing of "Blue Jay, Hop" and the resultant square dancing can be cut out without materially damaging the entity of the whole. If such cutting is to be effected, it might very well begin after Lincoln's line: "How about a *song* for the happy pair?" The others can voice approval, even applaud; and Sis can say: "That's a good idea, Mr. Lincoln. Come on into the parlor, everybody. We must get on with our practicin', anyways." She then leads the way upstage and stands near kitchen door while all of the other women file out UR, as in the present script.

THE PROPERTIES

On Stage

    lighted lamp (on table C)
    basket of knitting (on settee RC)
    logs (in fireplace DR)
    brass bed-warmer (standing against fireplace)
    * "Missouri Harmony Book" (Sis Beaseley, behind table)

Brought On

    plate of food, knife, fork, spoon (Sis, from UR)
    wooden pail (Nate, from ULC)
    handkerchief, watch, and fob (Judge Davis, from upstairs L)
    stovepipe hat, legal papers (Lincoln, from ULC)
    black reticule, pitch pipe (Miss Sophrony, from ULC)
    handkerchiefs and 4 "Missouri Harmony Books" (Miss Sophrony,
      Mrs. Jackson, Luly May, and Keenie; from ULC)

---

* (Note: The "Missouri Harmony Book" was a fairly large ledger-type book, about eleven inches wide by only eight inches high.)

"NEW SALEM"

Words from Missourri Harmony Book
Music by CHASE WEBB

Oh, Thou in whose presence my soul takes de—light, On

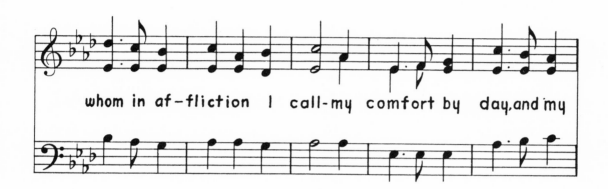

whom in af—fliction I call—my comfort by day, and my

song in the night, my hope, my sal —va—tion, my all!

"OLD BLUE JAY" - Schottische

Words and Music by CHASE WEBB

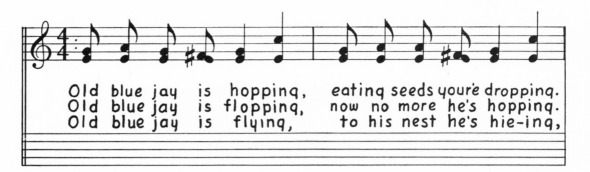

Old blue jay is hopping,   eating seeds you're dropping.
Old blue jay is flopping,   now no more he's hopping.
Old blue jay is flying,   to his nest he's hie-ing,

Your corn will nev-er grow.   Old blue jay is merry,
My corn is sure to grow.   Old blue jay's a smarty.
now that his day is thru.   Old blue jay is merry,

eats all he can carry, hopping down the   row.   Hop, blue jay!
but this is no party, old blue jay must   go.   Flop, blue jay!
has all he can carry; that goes for me   too! (END)

Here's a clod for you. Hop, blue jay! Eating time is through!
Go on flop a-way; flop, blue jay! This is not your day!

APPENDIX II

Lists of plays, musicals, and plays for a child audience. The lists include titles recommended by the Secondary School Theatre Conference, a division of the American Educational Theatre Association.

Catalogues in which all these shows are described can be obtained free of charge from the publishers listed in Chapter II.

LONG PLAYS

Abe Lincoln in Illinois
Adding Machine, The
Admirable Crichton, The
Ah, Wilderness!
All My Sons
Amahl and the Night Visitors
Anastasia
Androcles and the Lion
Angel Street
Animal Farm
Antigone—Sophocles
Antigone—Anouilh
Any Number Can Die

Arms and the Man
Around the World in 80 Days
Arsenic and Old Lace
As You Like It
Bad Seed, The
Barefoot in Athens
Barefoot in the Park
Barretts of Wimpole Street, The
Beggar on Horseback
Bell for Adano, A
Belles on Their Toes
Benten the Thief
Berkeley Square
Best Foot Forward
Best Laid Plans, The

Beyond the Fringe
Beyond the Horizon
Billy Budd
Billy Liar
Blithe Spirit
Blue Denim
Boast of the Town
Boy Who Changed the World, The
Bury the Dead
Caine Mutiny Court-Martial, The
Calamity Jane
Calculated Risk
Career Angel
Case of Libel, A
Cave Dwellers, The
Celebration
Chalk Garden, The
Charley's Aunt
Cheaper by the Dozen
Child Buyer, The
Clearing in the Woods, A
Comedy of Errors
Company of Wayward Saints, The
Cook for Mr. General, A
Corn Is Green, The
Corruption in the Palace of Justice
Cradle Song
Crucible, The
Curious Savage, The
Dark at the Top of the Stairs, The
Dark of the Moon
Darkness at Noon
David Copperfield
Dear Brutus
Dear Me, the Sky Is Falling

Dear Ruth
Death Takes a Holiday
Deputy, The
Devil's Disciple, The
Diary of Anne Frank
Different Drummer
Dinny and the Witches
Dirty Work at the Crossroads
Dream World
Drunkard, The, or The Fallen Saved
Egg and I, The
Eight Women—and a Ghost
Elizabeth the Queen
Enemy of the People, An
Enter Laughing
Everyman
Exit the Body
Family Nobody Wanted, The
Family Portrait
Fantasticks, The
Far Country, The
Father Knows Best
Father Malachy's Miracle
Father of the Bride
Firebugs, The
Five-Finger Exercise
Fool, The
Gammer Gurton's Needle
Gazebo, The
George Washington Slept Here
Glass Menagerie, The
Gold in the Hills
Golden Fleecing
Good-Bye My Fancy
Gramercy Ghost
Grass Harp, The
Great Big Doorstep
Great Expectations

Green Grow the Lilacs
Green Pastures, The
Guilty Party
Happiest Millionaire, The
Happy Time, The
Harriet
Harvey
Hasty Heart, The
Hay Fever
He Who Gets Slapped
Heiress, The
High Tor
Highest Tree, The
Hollow Crown, The
Home Is the Hunter
Home Sweet Homicide
Hostile Witness
House of Bernarda Alba, The
I Remember Mama
Inherit the Wind
Imaginary Invalid, The
Importance of Being Earnest, The
Innocent One, The
In White America
January Thaw
J.B.
Jenny Kissed Me
Junior Miss
Kind Lady
Kingdom of God, The
Kiss for Cinderella, A
Kiss Mama
Ladies of the Jury
Ladies of the Soissons, The
Lady Precious Stream
Lark, The
Late Christopher Bean, The
Laura

Leading Lady
Letters to Lucerne
Life With Father
Life With Mother
Liliom
Little Moon of Alban
Little Women
Look Homeward, Angel
Lord Pengo
Lost Horizon
Love Is Eternal
Love Out of Town
Lullaby
Macbeth
Madwoman of Chaillot, The
Magnificent Yankee, The
Majority of One, A
Male Animal, The
Man Called Peter, A
Man for All Seasons, A
Man Who Came to Dinner, The
Marriage Wheel
Mary of Scotland
Mary Rose
Matchmaker, The
Medea
Meet Me in St. Louis
Merchant Gentleman, The
Midsummer Night's Dream, A
Minor Miracle
Miracle Worker, The
Miser, The
Mr. Pim Passes By
Mrs. McThing
Moby Dick—Rehearsed
Mouse That Roared, The
Mousetrap, The
Much Ado About Nothing
Murder in the Cathedral

Murder Has Been Arranged, A
Murder on the Nile
My Heart's in the Highlands
My Sister Eileen
My Three Angels
Night of January 16, The
Night Must Fall
1984
Noah
No Crime in the Streets
On Borrowed Time
Ondine
Onions in the Stew
Only an Orphan Girl
Our Hearts Were Young and Gay
Our Town
Out of the Frying Pan
Outward Bound
Papa Is All
People vs. Maxine Lowe, The
Phedre
Philadelphia, Here I Come!
Physicists, The
Playroom, The
Pocket Watch, The
Portrait of Jennie
Pride and Prejudice
Prologue to Glory
Pure as the Driven Snow; or A Working Girl's Secret
Pursuit of Happiness, The
Pygmalion
Quality Street
Rainmaker, The
Raisin in the Sun, A
Ralph Roister Doister
Ramshackle Inn
Ransom

Rebel Without a Cause
Red Shoes, The
Remarkable Incident at Carson Corners, The
Remarkable Mr. Pennypacker, The
Rhinoceros
Ring Around the Moon
Rivalry, The
Rivals, The
Romancers, The
Romeo and Juliet
Room Full of Roses
Royal Hunt of the Sun
R. U. R.
Saint Joan
School for Husbands
School for Scandal, The
See How They Run
Seidman and Son
Send Me No Flowers
Servant in the House
Servant of Two Masters, The
Seven Nuns at Las Vegas
Seven Sisters
Shadow and Substance
She Stoops to Conquer
Silver Whistle, The
Skin of Our Teeth, The
Solid Gold Cadillac, The
Song of Bernadette
Stage Door
Stalag-17
Stardust
Star-Wagon
State Fair
Stephen D.
Streets of New York, The
Strife

Subject Was Roses, The
Sunrise at Campobello
Swan, The
Take Her, She's Mine!
Taming of the Shrew, The
Tavern, The
Teahouse of the August Moon,
  The
Tempest, The
Ten Little Indians
Theatre of Peretz, The
Thieves' Carnival
Thunder on Sycamore Street
Thurber Carnival, A
Tiger at the Gates
Time Out for Ginger
Tom Jones
Treasures on Earth
Trojan Women, The
Trophy for Mr. Heartfelt
Twelfth Night
Twelve Angry Men
Uncle Vanya
Under Milkwood
UTBU
Visit to a Small Planet
Warrior's Husband, The
Watch It, Sailor
Watch on the Rhine
What a Life
What Every Woman Knows
We're All Guilty
We Shook the Family Tree
White House, The
White Steed, The
Winslow Boy, The
Wings of the Dove, The
Winterset
Witness for the Prosecution

Wizard of Oz
World of Carl Sandburg, The
World of Sholom Aleichim, The
Would-be Gentleman, The
Years Ago
Yellow Jacket, The
You Can't Kiss Caroline
You Can't Take It With You
You, the Jury
Young and Beautiful, The
Young and Fair, The
Youngest, The
Your Every Wish

SHORT PLAYS

Ah, Cruel Fate!
Ali's Barbara
Apollo of Bellac, The
Aria da Capo
Bad Children, The
Bald Soprano, The
Benito Cereno
Birthday of the Infanta, The
Blind, The
Boor, The
Box and Cox
Boy With a Cart
Brick and the Rose, The
Case of the Crushed Petunias,
  The
Chairs, The
Claw, The
Cup of Tea, A
Curse You, Jack Dalton
Dear Departed, The
Death of the Hired Man, The
Devil and Daniel Webster, The
Doctor in Spite of Himself, The

Dope
Drapes Come, The
Dust of the Road
Early Frost
Ethel and Albert Comedies
Farce of the Worthy Master Pierre Patelin, The
Feathertop
Finders-Keepers
Fixin's
Fumed Oak
Genesis
Great Career, A
Happy Journey to Trenton and Camden, The
Hello, Out There
High Window
Hope is the Thing With Feathers
If Men Played Cards as Women Do
'Ile
Impromptu
Informer, The
In the Zone
Joint Owners in Spain
Last of the Lowries, The
Lost Silk Hat, The
Lawyer Lincoln
Lesson, The
Littlest Angel, The
Long Christmas Dinner, The
Lottery, The
Maker of Dreams, The
Man Who Died at Twelve O'Clock, The
Manikin and Minikin
Marriage Proposal, The
Medea

Monkey's Paw, The
Mooncalf Mugford
My Kinsman, Major Molineux
Neighbors, The
No 'Count Boy, The
Not Enough Rope
Old Lady Shows Her Medals, The
Once Upon a Playground
One Day in the Life of Ivan Denisovich
One Egg
Other Wise Man, The
Overtones
Parted on Her Wedding Morn
Partridge in a Pear Tree, A
Pedestrian, The
Plum Tree, The
Poor Aubrey
Prize Play, The
Queens of France
Red Carnations
Riders to the Sea
Romancers, The
Sandbox, The
Scrooge
Seeds of Suspicion
Seven Women
Shall We Join the Ladies?
Six New Plays In-the-Round
Sorry, Wrong Number
Sounds of Triumph
Sparkin'
Spreading the News
Stolen Prince, The
Storm Is Breaking, A
Suburban Tragedy
Sunday Costs Five Pesos

Sunny Morning, A
This Property Is Condemned
Trifles
Trysting Place, The
Twelve-Pound Look, The
Two Crooks and a Lady
Ugly Duckling, The
Valiant, The
Who-Ho Within!
Where the Cross Is Made
Why the Chimes Rang
Wisp in the Wind
Wonder Hat, The
Workhouse Ward, The
York Nativity Play, The
Young Lady of Property, A

MUSICALS

All In Love
Allegro
Amorous Flea, The
Annie Get Your Gun
Anything Goes
Babes in Arms
Baker Street
Barefoot Boy With Cheek
Bells Are Ringing
Boy Friend, The
Boys From Syracuse, The
Brigadoon
By Hex
Bye-Bye, Birdie!
Camelot
Carmen Jones
Carnival!
Carousel

Cinderella
Cindy
Damn Yankees
Earnest in Love
Fashion; or Life in New York
Fiddler on the Roof
Finian's Rainbow
Fiorello!
First Impressions
Flower Drum Song
Funny Girl
Gentlemen Prefer Blondes
Girl Crazy
Goldilocks
Guys and Dolls
Half a Sixpence
High Button Shoes
How to Succeed in Business
    Without Really Trying
I Married an Angel
Jo
King and I, The
Kismet
Kiss Me, Kate!
Legend of Sleepy Hollow
L'il Abner
Little Mary Sunshine
Little Me
Lute Song, The
Me and Juliet
Most Happy Fella
Music Man, The
My Fair Lady
No, No, A Million Times No!
    or Only a Farmer's Daughter
Of Thee I Sing
Oklahoma!
Oliver!

On a Clear Day You Can See
    Forever
Once Upon a Mattress
110 in the Shade
Pajama Game
Peter Pan
Pipe Dream
Plain and Fancy
Red Mill
Riverwind
Secret Life of Walter Mitty, The
Seventeen
Show Boat
Sing Out Sweet Land!
Skyscraper
Sound of Music, The
South Pacific
Stephen Foster, or Weep No
    More My Ladies
Streets of New York, The
Superman
Thirteen Clocks
Triad
West Side Story
Where's Charley?
Wildcat
Wonderful Town
Young Abe Lincoln

JUNIOR HIGH— CHILDREN'S PLAYS

Abe Grew Tall or Abe Lincoln
    of Pigeon Creek
Abe Lincoln—New Salem Days
Adventures of Tom Sawyer, The
Aladdin and the Wonderful
    Lamp
Ali Baba and the Forty Thieves

Alice in Wonderland
Androcles and the Lion
Arthur and the Magic Sword
Bachelor and the Bobby-Soxer,
    The
Bad Children, The
Beauty and the Beast
Big Klaus and Little Klaus
Black Widow, The
Brave Little Tailor, The
Buffalo Bill
Canterville Ghost, The
Case for Two Detectives
Cat on the Oregon Trail, The
Children, The
Christmas Carol, A
Christmas Nightingale, The
Cinderella
Clown Who Ran Away, The
Crazy Cricket Farm
Cricket on the Hearth, The
Crying Princess and the Golden
    Goose, The
Dancing Donkey, The
Dancing Princesses, The
Daniel Boone
Davy Crockett and His Coonskin
    Cap
Dick Whittington and His Cat
Don Quixote of La Mancha
Elves and the Shoemaker, The
Emperor's New Clothes, The
Emperor's Nightingale, The
Enchanted Treasure, The
Five Little Peppers
Flibbertygibbet, His Last Chance
Fool's Paradise
Footfalls
Fox in a Fix

Frog Princess and the Witch, The
Ghost of Mr. Penny, The
Good Witch of Boston, The
Great Cross-Country Race, The
   or
The Hare and the Tortoise
Greensleeves' Magic
Hans Brinker and the Silver
   Skates
Hansel and Gretel
Honorable Aladdin
Haunting of Hill House, The
Heidi
Hiawatha, Peacemaker of the
   Iroquois
Huckleberry Finn
Indian Captive: The Story of
   Mary Jemison
Jack and the Beanstalk
Joan of Arc
Johnny Moonbeam and the Silver
   Arrow
King Arthur's Sword
King Midas and the Golden
   Touch
King of the Golden River, The
King Patch and Mr. Simpkins
Land of the Dragon, The
Lincoln's Secret Messenger
Little Lee Bobo or The China-
   town Detective
Little Red Riding Hood or
   Grandmother Slyboots
Little Shepherd, The
Little Women
Maggie's Magic Teapot
Magic Fish-Bone, The
Magic Horn of Charlemagne, The
Magic in the Sky

Man Who Killed Time, The
Many Moons
Marco Polo
Marvelous Land of Oz, The
Master Cat and 6 Other Plays,
   The
Meet the Folks
Melody Jones
Merry Pranks of Tyll, The
Miracle at Potter's Farm
Mr. Popper's Penguins
Mystery at the Old Fort
Mystery Rocket, The
National Velvet
Niccolo and Nicolette
Nobody's Boy—Remi's Secret
   Locket
No Dogs Allowed or Junket
Nuremberg Stove, The
Oliver Twist
Panda and the Spy, The
Pegora the Witch
Peter, Peter, Pumpkin Eater or
   Bean Blossom Hill
Pied Piper of Hamelin, The
Pinocchio
Pioneers in Petticoats (a
   collection)
Plain Princess, The
Pocahontas
Prince Fairfoot
Prince and the Pauper, The
Princess and the Swineherd, The
Pyramus and Thisbe
Rabbit Who Wanted Red Wings,
   The
Radio Rescue
Rags to Riches
Rama and the Tigers

Ramshackle Inn

Rapunzel and the Witch

Red Shoes, The

Reynard the Fox

Rip Van Winkle

Robin Hood

Robinson Crusoe

Rumplestiltskin

Sandalwood Box, The

Secret of Han Ho, The

Seven Little Rebels

Simple Simon or Simon Big Ears

Sinbad the Sailor

Sleeping Beauty, The

Snow Girl, The

Snow Queen and the Goblin, The

Snow White and the Seven
  Dwarfs

Tall Tales (a collection)

Tevya and His Daughters

Three Bears, The

Three Thousand Mice of Dr.
  Proctor, The

Tinder Box, The

Tom Edison and the Wonderful
  Why

Tom Sawyer

Travelers, The

Trudi and the Minstrel

Two Pails of Water

Tyl Eulenspiegel and the Talking
  Donkey

Unwicked Witch, The

William Tell

Witch's Lullaby, The

Wizard of Oz, The

Whodunit?

Wonderful Tang, The

Young Ben

Young Dick Whittington

Young Hickory

Your Every Wish

BIBLIOGRAPHY

Books on Production

Adix, Vern. *Theatre Scenecraft: For the Backstage Technician and Artist*. Anchorage, Ky.: Children's Theatre Press, 1956.

Buerki, Frederick A. *Stagecraft for Nonprofessionals*. Madison: University of Wisconsin, 1945.

Davis, Jed H., Mary Jane Watkins, Roger M. Busfield, Jr. *Children's Theatre: Play Production for the Child Audience*. New York: Harper and Row, 1950.

Friederich, Willard J., John H. Fraser. *Scenery Design for the Amateur Stage*. New York: Macmillan, 1950.

Gassner, John. *Producing the Play: with The New Scene Technician's Handbook by Philip Barber*. New York: Dryden, 1953.

Hake, Herbert V. *Here's How: A Basic Stagecraft Book*. Evanston, Ill.: Row Peterson, 1958.

Nelms, Henning. *Play Production*. New York: Barnes and Noble, 1958.

Ommanney, Katherine Anne. *The Stage and the School*. New York: McGraw-Hill, 1960.

Selden, Samuel, editor. *Organizing a Community Theatre*. New York: Theatre Arts Books, 1945.

Simon's Directory of Theatrical Materials, Services and Information. New York: Package Publicity Service, 1963.

Books on Directing

Brown, Gilmore, Alice Garwood. *General Principles of Play Direction.* New York: Samuel French, 1936.

Canfield, Curtis. *The Craft of Play Directing.* New York: Holt, Rinehart and Winston, 1963.

Cole, Toby, Helen Krich Chinoy. *Directors on Directing.* Indianapolis: Bobbs-Merrill, 1963.

Dean, Alexander. *The Fundamentals of Play Directing.* New York: Holt, Rinehart and Winston, 1965.

Dietrich, John E. *Play Direction.* Englewood Cliffs, N.J.: Prentice-Hall, 1953.

Gallaway, Marian. *The Director in the Theatre.* New York: Macmillan, 1963.

Gielgud, John. *Stage Directions.* New York: Random House, 1963.

Hughes, Glenn. *The Penthouse Theatre: Its History and Technique.* Seattle: University of Washington, 1958.

Klein, Ruth. *The Art and Technique of Play Directing.* New York: Rinehart and Co., 1953.

Latham, Jean Lee. *Do's and Don'ts of Drama: 555 Pointers for Beginning Actors and Directors.* Chicago: Dramatic Publishing Co., 1935.

Simos, Jack. *Social Growth Through Play Production.* New York: Association Press, 1957.

Books on Acting

Boleslavsky, Richard. *Acting: The First Six Lessons*. New York: Theatre Arts Books, 1933.

Duerr, Edwin. *The Length and Depth of Acting*. New York: Holt, Rinehart and Winston, 1962.

Lewis, Robert. *Method or Madness?* New York: Samuel French, 1958.

McGaw, Charles. *Acting Is Believing: A Basic Method for Beginners*. New York: Holt, Rinehart and Winston, 1966.

Oxenford, Lyn. *Playing Period Plays*. London: J. Garnet Miller, 1955. Cloth or paper.

Redgrave, Michael. *Mask or Face: Reflections in an Actor's Mirror*. New York: Theatre Arts Books, 1958.

Savan, Bruce. *Your Career in the Theatre*. Garden City, N.Y.: Doubleday, 1961.

Selden, Samuel. *First Steps in Acting, Second Edition*. New York: Appleton-Century-Crofts, 1964.

Spolin, Viola. *Improvisation for the Theatre: A Handbook of Teaching and Directing Techniques*. Evanston, Ill.: Northwestern University, 1963.

Stanislavsky, Constantin S. *An Actor Prepares*. New York: Theatre Arts, 1936.

Stanislavsky, Constantin S. *Building a Character*. New York: Theatre Arts, 1949.

Stanislavsky, Constantin. *My Life in Art*. New York: Theatre Arts, 1924. Cloth or paper.

Books on Theatre People

Allen, Steve. *Mark It and Strike It: An Autobiography*. New York: Holt, Rinehart and Winston, 1960.

Brown, Ivor. *Shaw in His Time*. London: Thomas Nelson, 1965.

Cole, Toby, Helen Crich Chinoy, editors. *Actors On Acting: The Theories, Techniques, and Practices of the Great Actors of All Times as Told in Their Own Words*. New York: Crown, 1949.

Davis, Sammy, Jane and Burt Boyar. *Yes, I Can*. New York: Farrar, Straus and Giroux, 1965.

Day, Donald. *Will Rogers*. New York: David McKay, 1962.

Funke, Lewis, John E. Booth. *Actors Talk About Acting: Fourteen Interviews With Stars of the Theatre*. New York: Random House, 1961. Cloth or paper.

Guthrie, Tyrone. *A Life in the Theatre*. New York: McGraw-Hill, 1959. Cloth or paper.

Hardwicke, Sir Cedric, as told to James Brough. *A Victorian in Orbit: Irreverent Memoirs of Sir Cedric Hardwicke*. Garden City, N.Y.: Doubleday, 1961.

Hart, Moss. *Act One*. New York: Modern Library, 1959. Cloth or paper.

Horne, Lena, Richard Schickel. *Lena*. New York: Doubleday, 1965.

Kerr, Laura. *Footlights to Fame: The Life of Fanny Kemble*. New York: Funk and Wagnalls, 1962.

Langner, Lawrence. *The Magic Curtain*. New York: E. P. Dutton, 1951.

Lee, Gypsy Rose. *Gypsy.* New York: Harper and Row, 1957. Cloth or paper.

Malvern, Gladys. *Curtain Going Up! The Story of Katharine Cornell.* New York: Julian Messner, 1943.

Murray, Marian. *Circus! From Rome to Ringling.* New York: Appleton Century-Crofts, 1956.

Sherman, Allan. *A Gift of Laughter.* New York: Atheneum, 1965.

Skinner, Cornelia Otis. *Madame Sarah.* Boston: Houghton Mifflin, 1967.

Tynan, Kenneth. *Alec Guinness.* London: Barrie and Rockliff, 1961.

Wagenknecht, Edward. *Seven Daughters of the Theatre.* Norman: University of Oklahoma, 1964.

Wagner, Frederick, Barbara Brady. *Famous American Actors and Actresses.* New York: Dodd, Mead, 1961.

Wallace, Irving. *The Fabulous Showman: The Life and Times of P. T. Barnum.* New York: Alfred A. Knopf, 1959.

Waters, Ethel, with Charles Samuels. *His Eye Is on the Sparrow.* New York: Bantam, 1950.

Wood, Peggy. *Arts and Flowers.* New York: William Morrow, 1963.

Zolotow, Maurice. *Stagestruck: The Romance of Alfred Lunt and Lynn Fontanne.* New York: Harcourt, Brace and World, 1965.

BOOKS ON SHAKESPEARE

Beckerman, Bernard. *Shakespeare at the Globe: 1599-1609.* New York: Macmillan, 1962. Cloth or paper.

Berman, Ronald. *A Reader's Guide to Shakespeare's Plays: A Discursive Bibliography*. Chicago: Scott, Foresman, 1965.

Boas, Guy. *Shakespeare and the Young Actor*. London: Dufour, 1955.

Brown, Ivor. *Shakespeare in His Time*. London: Thomas Nelson, 1960.

Chute, Marchette. *Shakespeare of London*. New York: E. P. Dutton, 1949.

Chute, Marchette. *Stories From Shakespeare*. New York: New American Library, 1962.

de Banke, Cécile. *Shakespearean Stage Production Then and Now*. New York: Hutchinson, 1954.

Granville-Barker, Harley. *Preface to Hamlet*. New York: Hill and Wang, 1946.

Holzknecht, Karl J. *The Background of Shakespeare's Plays*. Lancaster, Texas: American Book Company, 1950.

Hudson, A. K. *Shakespeare and the Classroom*. London: Heinemann, 1963.

Kerman, Gertrude Lerner, *Shakespeare for Young Players: From Tens to Teens*. Irvington-on-Hudson, N.Y.: Harvey House, 1964.

Kott, Jan. *Shakespeare Our Contemporary*. Garden City, N.Y.: Doubleday, 1964. Cloth or paper.

Norman, Charles. *The Playmaker of Avon*. New York: David McKay, 1949.

Miller, Katherine. *Five Plays from Shakespeare*. Boston: Houghton Mifflin, 1964.

Price, George R. *Reading Shakespeare's Plays*. New York: Barron's, 1962.

Purdom, C. B. *What Happens in Shakespeare*. London: John Barker, 1963.

Reese, M. M. *William Shakespeare*. New York: St. Martin's, 1963.

Webster, Margaret. *Shakespeare Without Tears*. Boston: Fawcett, 1942.

BOOKS ON THEATRE HISTORY

Allen, John. *Masters of European Drama*. London: Dennis Dobson, 1962.

Brockett, Oscar G. *The Theatre: An Introduction*. New York: Holt, Rinehart and Winston, 1964.

Burton, E. J. *The Student's Guide to World Theatre*. New York: London House, 1962.

Cheney, Sheldon. *The Theatre: Three Thousand Years of Drama, Acting and Stagecraft*. New York: David McKay, 1952.

Clarke, R. F. *The Growth and Nature of Drama*. London: Cambridge University, 1965.

Clurman, Harold. *The Fervent Years: The Story of the Group Theatre and the Thirties*. New York: Hill and Wang, 1957.

Flanagan, Hallie. *Arena: The History of the Federal Theatre*. New York: Benjamin Blom, 1965.

Freedley, George, John A. Reeves. *A History of the Theatre*. New York: Crown, 1955.

Houghton, Norris. *Moscow Rehearsals: The Golden Age of the Soviet Theatre*. New York: Grove, 1962.

Hughes, Glenn. *A History of the American Theatre 1700-1950*. New York: Samuel French, 1951.

Hunt, Hugh. *The Live Theatre: An Introduction to the History and Practice of the Stage*. New York: Oxford, 1962.

Jolliffe, H. R. *Tales From the Greek Drama*. Philadelphia: Chilton, 1962.

Joseph, Stephen. *The Story of the Playhouse in England*. London: Barrie and Rockliff, 1963.

Mander, Raymond, Joe Mitchenson. *A Picture History of the British Theatre*. London: Macmillan, 1962.

Marek, Hannelore. *The History of the Theatre*. New York: Odyssey Press, 1964.

Morris, Lloyd. *Curtain Time: The Story of the American Theatre*. New York: Random House, 1953.

Priestley, J. B. *The Wonderful World of the Theatre*. Garden City, N.Y.: Doubleday, 1959.

Simonson, Lee. *The Stage Is Set*. New York: Theatre Arts, 1963.

BOOKS ON APPRECIATION

Altshuler, Thelma and Richard Paul Janaro. *Responses to Drama*. New York: Houghton Mifflin Co., 1967.

Brown, Ivor, *What Is a Play?* London: Macdonald, 1964.

Davis, Mike. *The Wonderful World of Ballet*. London: Odhams, 1965.

Ernst, Earle. *The Kabuki Theatre*. New York: Oxford, 1956.

Green, Stanley. *The World of Musical Comedy*. New York: Grosset and Dunlap, 1962.

Hatlen, Theodore W. *Orientation to the Theatre*. New York: Appleton-Century-Crofts, 1962.

Mearns, Hughes. *Creative Power: The Education of Youth in the Creative Arts*. New York: Dover, 1958.

Selden, Samuel. *Man in His Theatre*. Chapel Hill: University of North Carolina, 1957.

Styan, John Louis. *The Dramatic Experience: A Guide to the Reading of Plays*. London: Cambridge, 1965.

Styan, John Louis. *The Elements of Drama*. London: Cambridge, 1960. Cloth or paper.

Whiting, Frank M. *An Introduction to the Theatre*. New York: Harper and Row, 1954.

Wright, Edward A. *A Primer for Playgoers: An Introduction to the Understanding and Appreciation of Cinema-Stage-Television*. Englewood Cliffs, N.J.: Prentice-Hall, 1958.

BOOKS ON PLAYWRITING

Busfield, Roger M., Jr. *The Playwright's Art: Stage, Radio, Television, Motion Pictures*. New York: Harper and Row, 1958.

McCalmon, George, Christian Moe. *Creating Historical Drama: A Guide for the Community and the Interested Individual*. Carbondale: Southern Illinois University Press, 1965.

MacGowan, Kenneth. *A Primer of Playwriting*. New York: Random House, 1951.

BOOKS ON SPEECH

Anderson, Virgil A. *Training the Speaking Voice*. New York: Oxford, 1961.

Copeland, Lewis. *The World's Great Speeches*. New York: Dover, 1958.

Lee, Charlotte I. *Oral Interpretation*. Boston: Houghton Mifflin, 1959.

Levy, Louis, Edward W. Mammen, Robert Sonkin. *Voice and Speech Handbook*. Englewood Cliffs, N.J.: Prentice-Hall, 1960.

McBurney, James H., Ernest J. Wragge. *The Art of Good Speech*. Englewood Cliffs, N.J.: Prentice-Hall, 1953.

Uris, Dorothy. *Everybody's Book of Better Speaking*. New York: David McKay, 1960.

BOOKS ON CONTEMPORARY THEATRE

Brustein, Robert. *The Theatre of Revolt: An Approach to the Modern Drama*. Boston: Little, Brown, 1964.

Corrigan, Robert W., editor. *Theatre in the Twentieth Century*. New York: Grove Press, 1963.

Ewen, Frederick. *Bertolt Brecht. His Life, His Art and His Times*. New York: Citadel, 1967.

Gassner, John. *Directions in Modern Theatre and Drama: An Expanded Edition of Form and Idea in Modern Theatre*. New York: Holt, Rinehart and Winston, 1965.

Guthrie, Tyrone. *In Various Directions*. New York: Macmillan, 1965.

Jones, Robert Edmond. *The Dramatic Imagination: Reflections and Speculations on the Art of the Theatre*. New York: Theatre Arts, 1941.

Kerr, Walter. *The Theatre in Spite of Itself*. New York: Simon and Schuster, 1963.

Rice, Elmer. *The Living Theatre*. New York: Harper and Brothers, 1959.

Wellwarth, George E. *The Theatre of Protest and Paradox: Developments in the Avant-Garde Drama*. New York: New York University, 1964. Cloth or paper.

Willett, John. *The Theatre of Bertolt Brecht*. Philadelphia: New Directions, 1959.

Books on the Mass Media

Calder-Marshall, Arthur. *The Innocent Eye: The Life of Robert J. Flaherty*. New York: Harcourt, Brace and World, 1963.

Hall, Stuart, Paddy Whannel. *The Popular Arts*. New York: Random House, 1965.

Kostelanetz, Richard, editor. *The New American Arts*. New York: Horizon, 1965.

McLuhan, Marshall. *Understanding Media: The Extension of Man*. New York: McGraw-Hill, 1965.

Ringgold, Gene. *The Films of Bette Davis*. New York: Citadel, 1966.

Rosenberg, Bernard, David Manning White, editors. *Mass Culture: The Popular Arts in America*. New York: Macmillan, 1964.

Swallow, Norman. *Factual Television*. New York: Hastings House, 1966.

Taylor, Deems, Bryant Hale. *A Pictorial History of the Movies.* New York: Simon and Schuster, 1949.

Wallace, Carlton. *Making Movies.* London, Evans, 1965.

BIBLIOGRAPHIES AND GUIDES

A Suggested Outline for a Course of Study in Theatre Arts: Secondary School Level. Washington, D.C.: American Educational Theatre Association, 1968.

Drury, F. K. W. *Drury's Guide to Best Plays.* New York: Scarecrow Press, 1953.

Shank, Theodore J., editor. *A Digest of 500 Plays: Plot Outlines and Production Notes.* New York: Crowell-Collier, 1963.

Shipley, Joseph T. *Guide to Great Plays.* Washington, D.C.: Public Affairs Press, 1956.

Sobel, Bernard. *The New Theatre Handbook and Digest of Plays.* New York: Crown, 1959.

Notes

Notes

Notes

Notes

Notes

Notes

Notes

Notes